A Future for Public Ownership

A Future for Public Ownership

Malcolm Sawyer and Kathy O'Donnell

Lawrence & Wishart
LONDON

Lawrence & Wishart Limited
99a Wallis Road
London E9 5LN

First published 1999

British Library Cataloguing in Publication data.
A catalogue record for this book is available from the British Library.

ISBN 0 85315 885 1

Typeset in North Wales by
Derek Doyle & Associates, Mold, Flintshire.
Printed and bound in Great Britain by
Redwood Books Limited, Trowbridge.

Contents

Preface

The annual conference of UNISON supported the view that the privatised utilities should be returned to public ownership. The report of the NEC of UNISON in 1996 summarised the position as follows:

> The composite motions adopted at last year's Conference go beyond the principle of ownership and control to the need to examine how they can be implemented within a reasonably detailed plan. Any proposal to return the utilities to public ownership and control, however, has to acknowledge that the electricity, gas and water utilities have undergone major change and are substantially different in organisation and structure to when they operated within the public sector. The legal and fiscal measures required will therefore be complex and the Parliamentary procedure somewhat lengthy' (UNISON, 1996, p. 16).

This book is the result of research commissioned by UNISON to elaborate proposals for the public ownership of the utilities. We have set out the major objectives of public ownership and evaluated the major obstacles to the achievement of public ownership. It also considers the alternative to public ownership - the continuing regulation of privatised utilities - and the problems which that presents. We conclude with an evaluation of six options for public ownership, looking at how they could be implemented.

We conclude that there are no insurmountable obstacles to the public ownership of the utilities, and that there are a range of feasible and attractive options for the implementation of that public ownership.

We are pleased to present our book as a contribution to the debates over the future of the utilities and to the arguments for public ownership.

Summary of Argument

Chapter 1 introduces the book. **Chapter 2** considers what public ownership could achieve. Public ownership would enable community control over key activities in the context of globalisation. It should enable standards of employment practice to be set and observed. Income distribution and environmental considerations are also relevant. Public ownership can achieve lower prices through a lower required rate of return on capital as compared with the private sector.

It is often argued that public ownership is inevitably inefficient, providing low quality services. This argument is examined in **Chapter 3** by reviewing the evidence on the comparative performance of public and private ownership and on the effects of the privatisation programme in the UK. The evidence does *not* support any general inferiority of public ownership as compared with private ownership in terms of efficiency, and that conclusion is reached without regard to the wider objectives of public ownership as compared with private ownership.

Chapter 4 considers regulation, which is the alternative to public ownership of the utilities. Regulation by its nature seeks to constrain, but not to develop. Effective regulation faces a range of difficulties. The regulatory agency may come to operate in the interests of the regulated rather than consumers or workers. The regulatory agency faces problems of collecting relevant information, and the ability of the regulatory agency to make meaningful comparisons is being eroded by mergers and diversification. The alternative modes of regulation of RPI - x and rate of return regulation are discussed.

Chapter 5 shows that the argument that public ownership is costly and would displace other worthy forms of public expenditure is essentially false. Expenditure on public ownership, unlike most other forms of public expenditure, generates revenue and profits for the government. Public ownership is financed by the issue of interest-bearing bonds, and the interest payments on the bonds can be met by the future profits of the public utility. The price paid for the companies taken into public ownership must not be an inflated one.

Based on legal opinion obtained by UNISON from Lord Wedderburn, it is concluded that there is no constitutional or other legal reason which would totally prohibit the government from bringing the utilities back into public ownership. The Treaty of Rome would not appear to create any major obstacles to public ownership.

The emerging structure of the utilities, such as vertical disintegration, competition in gas and electricity production, cross-ownership between sectors and diversification, may limit the possibilities for public ownership. These dimensions raise questions for the appropriate structure of the industries under public ownership, and which parts of those industries should be returned to public ownership. The nature of the ownership of the privatised utility companies, including that by financial institutions (notably pension funds) and by foreign owners, and also the extent to which the privatised utilities are wholly owned by other, notably foreign, companies, may also place constraints on public ownership.

Chapter 6 reviews a range of issues concerned with public and private ownership. The objectives of public ownership are more than simply the achievement of efficiency, but an inefficient and ineffective public sector would serve no-one's interests. Public ownership will have wider objectives than private ownership: ultimately the former is concerned with the promotion of the general social interest and the latter with profits.

One argument deployed in favour of private ownership is that it provides the incentive of profits to reduce costs and to promote efficient production. A second argument is that if a private company becomes lax, it will be punished by being taken over. A third argument is that competition promotes efficiency, that competition is usually associated with private rather than public ownership, and that competition is only effective when firms are struggling over profits. These arguments are found to be unconvincing.

Clear objectives should be established by Parliament for the publicly owned utilities in order to underpin their accountability. The salary structure within the public enterprise should strive to reduce inequalities. The vertical disintegration of utilities following privatisation has generated substantial transactions costs, and consideration of these costs should influence the structure for public ownership.

Two potential conflicting considerations arise with democratic participation in public enterprises. The management of public enterprise should be undertaken in an effective and innovative manner, with the managers and workers using their skills, talents and professional judgement to best effect, without external interference and meddling.

But public ownership should involve a degree of democratic control: the purpose of public ownership is ultimately to have an accountable and effective operation.

Six options for the form of public ownership are reviewed in **Chapter 7**. Those which involve complete public ownership would generally require the compulsory acquisition of the assets of the utilities, and future borrowing by the publicly owned utilities would be regarded as part of the public sector borrowing requirement (PSBR). Mutualisation and workers cooperatives would also probably require compulsory acquisition by the government.

Full public ownership would mean a vertically integrated national industry under public ownership, owned by the national government and accountable to Parliament. It is also taken to exclude the competitive provision of part of the production of the industry (e.g. electricity generation in the electricity industry), and the nationalised industry would be given a statutory monopoly.

Partial public ownership means that the company concerned would remain a separate entity, and not be a part of the state. The government receives dividends from the company which form part of the revenue of the government, but the company's accounts are consolidated with those of the government. Hence when the company borrows, it does so on its own account and on the basis of its own credit rating. This may well mean that it borrows at somewhat higher interest rates than the government would be able to do, but it also means that any borrowing is not regarded as part of the PSBR. Partial public ownership would not give the government or Parliament control over the company and regulation would still be required.

Strategic public ownership would involve the public ownership of some key elements such as the basic network within an industry. In the vertically disintegrated industries of electricity, gas and the railways, it is clearly feasible that what are regarded as key elements of those industries are brought back into public ownership, while other parts remain under private ownership or some mixture of public and private ownership.

The network is the key element in most of the utilities, and is the part of the system where the position of natural monopoly arises. Further, there is often concern over the safety of the network and who can have access to the network. Thus in the case of the railways, there is concern that the track, signalling, etc, meet safety requirements, and that the trains which run over the track are operated in a safe manner.

Regional public ownership could arise either through voluntary or compulsory acquisition. There are complications arising from the lack of coincidence between the boundaries of a region (or collection of local authorities) and those of the operations of the utility. A regional government could issue bonds, either in its own name or that of the acquired utility, and finance the acquisition from the proceeds. Depending on the financial powers given to the relevant regional authority by central government, it could well require permission by central government. It would, in effect, be possible to cede the regulatory function from the national regulatory bodies to the appropriate regional government.

The relevant government body in which ownership of the public enterprise would be lodged, and to whom it would be accountable, would have to be determined. Outside of England, the relevant tier of government would be the Scottish Parliament, or the Assemblies in Wales and Northern Ireland, but this would pose some difficulties in England in the absence of regional government. There would be a clear argument for mapping the geographical scope of the public enterprise with regional government if that came into being. In England, in the absence of regional government, regional public ownership would require the establishment of regional bodies which would oversee the regional enterprises, though the proposed Regional Development Agencies could be used for this purpose.

Mutualisation means that the company is owned collectively by its customers, with a share of the operating surplus of the company accruing to the customers. There are questions of how democratic these organisations have been and how much influence their members have on their operations. A clear danger of mutualisation is that customers have no influence over the management and decision-making of the mutual organisation and the management becomes self-perpetuating. There are clearly many examples of successful mutual organisations, at least in the sense that they have survived and prospered. It is also the case that the comparative performance of these organisations (that is compared with capitalist companies) has generally been good.

Mutual organisation generates two types of problem (which are echoed in the case of worker co-operatives). The first is that their rate of investment and rate of growth are limited by the available finance from their operating surplus, as mutual organisations typically finance their own expansion. The government may have to stand ready to lend to a mutualised utility. The second arises from the growth of the mutual organisation over time, so that it accrues capital assets which are owned by the mutual organisation and hence by the members collectively. There may be considerable surpluses accrued by the mutual organisation, which can be 'unlocked' by the current members if the organisation de-mutualises.

Mutualisation would require the re-acquisition of the now privatised company, probably by the government, and then their handing over to the customers of the company. It is possible to conceive of a compulsory capital levy on customers. The payment of dividends to customers would give them a 'double interest' in the company and its efficient operation, as customers and as owners. The mutual organisation should provide an identification between the company and the region which it serves and provide a form of regional autonomy.

A **workers' co-operative**, a form of **democratic employee ownership**, could operate at the local, regional or national level. The key attribute of a workers' co-operative is that the workers are the collective owners of the enterprise and as such have title to the net revenue of the enterprise, which may be divided into wages, workers' dividend or retained surplus to finance investment in capital equipment.

One of the key decisions of the workers collectively is the division of the net revenue of their co-operative between immediate income (wages plus workers' dividend) and investment in capital expenditure and expansion intended to provide additional future income. The basis on which that surplus is shared out among the workers varies. It may be proportional to their wage, it may be proportional to their own capital stake in the co-operative, it may be on a *per capita* basis. Workers' co-operatives can be financed by borrowing on a non-equity basis or by the use of the workers' own funds. The formal control of a workers' co-operative rests with the workers, usually on the basis of one worker one vote. In place of the board of directors elected by shareholders in a capitalist firm, there can be elections of directors by the workers. The establishment of workers' co-operatives would probably require the compulsory acquisition of the utilities by the government, followed by transfer to the workers. The workers would collectively have to pay interest on the bonds issued.

The general conclusions of this book are that there are no insurmountable economic or legal obstacles to the public ownership of utilities. Each of the six options examined is feasible, though with different balances of advantages and disadvantages. Different options are likely to be appropriate for different industries.

1

INTRODUCTION

This book examines the case for the extension of public ownership and in particular the public ownership of the major utilities. It looks in some detail at the major options for the extension of social ownership, ranging from re-nationalisation along the lines of the Morrisonian nationalised industries through to the establishment of mutual organisation and workers' co-operatives.

Many reasons lie behind the advocacy of public ownership, and some of the major reasons are examined in Chapter 2. These range from the exercise of community control through environmental considerations to distributional objectives.

Many would argue that public ownership is inevitably inefficient and provides low quality services, and that private ownership of the utilities provides the goods and services at lower costs. This argument is examined in Chapter 3 by reviewing the now extensive evidence on the comparative performance of public and private ownership and the more limited evidence on the effects of the privatisation programme in the UK. The evidence does *not* support any notion of the inferiority of public ownership, a conclusion reached even without regard to the wider objectives of public ownership compared with private ownership.

Regulation of privatised utilities is the main alternative to public ownership. Chapter 4 examines the problems of regulation, and questions whether or not regulation can deliver.

Chapter 5 reviews the obstacles to public ownership. It is suggested there that the widely used argument that it could not be afforded, or that if it could it would be at the expense of education and health services, is false. There are some legal pitfalls which need to be avoided, and legislation for public ownership is likely to be complex. The emerging diversified and vertically disintegrated structure of the privatised utilities presents some questions on the form and structure which public ownership should take.

In Chapter 6 we examine a range of issues relating to public ownership. We look critically at the theoretical arguments for the superiority of private ownership and on the role of competition. We also wish to draw lessons from the previous experience of public ownership for the setting of objectives for public enterprises and for the relationship between public enterprise and the democratic institutions.

Six options for public ownership are reviewed in Chapter 7. These are: full public ownership (or nationalisation), which would involve 100 per cent ownership; partial public ownership, with the government taking a substantial stake in the utilities; strategic public ownership; regional public ownership; mutualisation, under which consumers become the collective owners of the utility companies; and democratic employee ownership. While we conclude that all of these options are viable, we also consider their relative advantages and disadvantages.

Although we use the term public ownership throughout, it will be seen that some of the options considered may be described as social ownership – workers' co-operatives, and (consumer) mutual organisations – in which ownership is a collective one on behalf of the workers and consumers respectively. In workers' co-operatives and mutual organisations, the workers and consumers respectively have the legal rights to the surplus generated by their organisation. The ownership of the assets may be held elsewhere, e.g. by the government, or may be held collectively by the workers and consumers respectively. The term 'public ownership' is in general used rather than nationalisation as we would take the latter to be public ownership by the national government, whereas we wish to consider here a variety of forms of public ownership including ownership by local and regional government.

Public ownership is often associated with the nationalised industries which were organised as vertically integrated statutory monopolies. These firms were protected from competition from other companies, whether privately or publicly owned, but were themselves generally prohibited from diversification into other product areas. But there were other publicly owned companies which were in competition with privately owned companies and which were not vertically integrated (e.g. British Airways). Other companies (e.g. BP) were also partially owned by the government as well as being in competition with other firms. In this book we wish to consider a wide range of options for the structure of public ownership.

Much of the discussion in this book is quite broad, relating to public ownership in general. However, the particular concern of UNISON is with the public ownership of a range of industries, namely gas, electricity and water. We will use the term utilities to refer to these three industries plus the railways.

There are a few technical terms in the book. 'Natural monopoly' refers to a case in which it would be wasteful to have more than one producer because that would involve unnecessary duplication. One of the characteristics of the utilities is that they have distributional networks, and the provision of more than one network (rail links, electricity wires, gas pipes etc.) would be wasteful. It is worth noting that only part of the industries concerned constitute natural monopolies (the network) while other parts (e.g. operating a train, generating electricity) do not.

'Economies of scale' refers to the situation in which the unit costs of production decline as the scale of production rises. The scale of output at which economies of scale are essentially exhausted (often referred to as the 'minimum efficient scale') is particularly significant. When the minimum efficient scale is substantial relative to the size of the market, then one (or at most a few) enterprises producing at that scale are indicated.

'Economies of scope' refers to a situation in which undertaking two activities together is less costly than undertaking the two activities separately. For example, billing and meter reading for gas and for electricity may be subject to economies of scope, that is it is cheaper to undertake the two activities together rather than separately. Clearly when there are economies of scope, it would be cost effective to undertake the two activities together.

The extent to which there are network effects, economies of scale and of scope should clearly influence the precise structure of the industry concerned. But while the structure of the industry may be influenced by these factors, it is a separate matter whether or not the industry should be privately or publicly owned and accountable.

2

What can public ownership achieve?

Introduction

In this chapter we consider the reasons which lie behind proposals for public ownership. We set out what we see to be three main reasons for, and the objectives of public ownership. First, it should form the basis on which public ownership is campaigned for. Second, the design of the form of public ownership should be influenced by the reasons why public ownership is being advocated. Third, setting out the stall in terms of the objectives helps to confront the issue of whether or not public ownership is the relevant policy tool. For example, many would argue that regulation of a privatised company can achieve many of the objectives of public ownership. But this can only be clarified by reference to the objectives and by a consideration of how well regulation can meet those objectives.

Public ownership has historically occurred in a wide variety of ways and for many different reasons. In some cases companies have been taken into public ownership in response to an immediate crisis (e.g. British Leyland in the 1970s) or as a policy imperative (e.g. in France with the nationalisation of Renault in 1945 as 'punishment' for the collaboration of the private owners with the German occupation). In others, public ownership has happened only after prolonged campaigns over decades and the failure of other policies: some notable examples here include the nationalisation of the coal industry and of the railways in Britain under the Attlee government (cf chapters on those industries in Millward and Singleton, 1995). But, as Millward (1997, p 210) points out, while some ailing industries were nationalised by the Attlee government, others, such as cotton and shipbuilding, were not.

The purpose of the rest of this chapter is to consider the reasons which have been advanced for public ownership, while recognising that public ownership occurs in response to a conjuncture of political forces and perceived problems and crises in specific industries. In general, we seek to present the positive reasons for the case for public ownership though we recognise that there are also negative reasons, namely the failures of private ownership and the problems of regulation of privatised monopolies. Indeed, political support for public ownership has often been strengthened by the perceived failures of private ownership.

There are several possible lines of reasoning on which an advocacy of public ownership might be based. They are divided here into eight strands: the commanding heights of the economy; issues of community control; employment standards; income and wealth distribution; environmental considerations; the costs of capital; and issues of regulation and regulatory failure. In each of these cases, the aim is seen to be a worthy objective, which could well be better served by public ownership than by private ownership.

COMMANDING HEIGHTS

The case for public ownership has often been viewed in terms of public control of the 'commanding heights' of the economy. The idea has been that there are some industries which are too important to leave to the vagaries of the private sector and of the market, and that the future course of the economy depends on these key industries. As some have put the matter: computer chips are more important than potato chips. Industries such as the power industries – coal, gas and electricity – have been viewed as vital for the process of industrialisation. In that sense, such industries were of strategic importance. But these and other industries were of strategic importance in the sense that a domestic supply would be vital in the event of war: government support for agriculture was often justified along these lines.

A related argument is that industries which make products which are vital for life, or at least for modern industrialised life, should be under public influence if not control and ownership. This idea was well expressed by Will Hutton when he wrote that:

> Electricity is not a commodity like a designer dress where an interruption of supply poses no wider consequences; it is a precondition for successful modern life. If the owner of the power and distribution system fails to maintain supply and so loses revenue, this is not just an issue for the shareholders of the enterprise. It is an issue for everyone. In economic terms, electricity is a public good. This means electricity

> companies – like water, gas and rail companies – cannot be run on the same commercial terms as firms in markets where there are many suppliers and the consequences of poor decision making are restricted to the firms themselves (*Observer*, 8 March 1998).

It can be noted that this was written in the context of power failures in Auckland, New Zealand following privatisation.

The term 'commanding heights' can be interpreted in many ways, but it does rest on the notion that some industries are more important than others. There can be little doubt that 'life as we know it' would not be possible without electricity, gas and water, and those industries are part of the commanding heights of any industrialised economy. The private sector will only supply those vital products if it is profitable for it to do so, whereas the public sector can and should supply those products, provided that their supply and consumption is deemed to be socially beneficial. The requirements of profitability place limits on the stringency of regulation of privatised utilities.

COMMUNITY CONTROL

A related reason for public ownership is that it enables the community as a whole to exercise some control over the provision of key goods and services. This is particularly relevant in a globalised economy where ownership of, and control over, companies cannot readily be retained within the nation under private ownership. It is already apparent that ownership and control of many of the regional electricity companies (RECs) has passed into the hands of foreign companies (see chapter 5). There may be mechanisms such as a 'golden share' held by the government (used in a number of cases in the early stages of privatisation to prevent take-overs of which the government did not approve), and the use of merger policy, to retain control of the utilities within the country, but such mechanisms have clearly not been used to date.

Competition is seen by some as the means through which the community can exercise control over business. In this context, the community is taken as synonymous with consumers, and it is assumed that consumers can, through shopping around, exercise (collectively) influence over business. Whatever the merits of that argument, it lacks conviction in the context of natural monopolies and natural oligopolies. It is difficult to conceive of consumers shopping around for different national grids for electricity, and even where there can be more than one firm (as in the case of electricity generation) the number of firms is likely to be small. Through 'shopping around', consumers can express preferences over what is available and search for lower prices, thereby putting downward pressure on prices. But the consumer cannot express preferences over the level of investment (and hence future provision), over the security of supply or over supply to remote areas. The regulation of the privatised utilities, in effect, recognises the significance of those arguments to some degree, albeit with little attention to the issue of investment.

Some community control can be provided through regulation (where this is interpreted in a broad sense, from control over prices and profits to regulations governing the contents of the product). But regulation suffers from the difficulty of ensuring that regulations are effective; and in addition they tend to be negative rather than positive. In other words, regulations can either say that action X cannot be done or that if action Y is undertaken then it must be done in a certain way. Regulations rarely say that action Z must be undertaken. In the context of public utilities, regulations can say that if electricity is distributed it must be done in specific ways and the price charged can be (indirectly) controlled. But the regulations cannot say that company A must distribute electricity, though they may say that if company A distributes electricity to some in a region, it must do so to all: the universal service provision requirement.

Community control raises the obvious issue of how that control could be exercised within the framework of public ownership. There are severe agency problems (further discussed in chapter 6), by which we mean that there are difficulties in constructing institutions through which the community at large can exert effective control. The managers of a public enterprise are in day to day charge, and have the relevant information and the power to make significant decisions. It is inevitably difficult for 'outsiders' to obtain the relevant information and to monitor decisions, apart from the question of whether or not they have the incentives to do so. There would need to be democratic institutions which have the ability to exercise community control, and mechanisms by which public enterprises report to and are accountable to the public.

STANDARDS OF EMPLOYMENT

It has often been recognised that employment practices in the public sector should meet high standards, and to some degree set an example for the private sector. There would seem little doubt that, whatever the shortcomings of the public sector in terms of the achievement of good employment practices, there has been a worsening of employment conditions in the privatised utilities. The deterioration of working conditions, and the threats to trade union recognition and employment, are indicated in UNISON (1996). Here, again, some of these standards of employment practice could be imposed by law: trade union recognition, periods of notice, minimum wages, etc. But others may be more difficult, for example the overall structure of wages, or the participation of workers in effective decision-making.

In our discussions below, we will be implicitly assuming that there should be high employment standards under public ownership. This is, of course, by no means inevitable. But it is an argument for the inclusion of the objective of good employment practices (which should be specified) in laws establishing public ownership and in the criteria by which public ownership is judged.

INCOME AND WEALTH DISTRIBUTION

Public ownership, especially of a relatively small sector of the economy, cannot be expected to have a major impact on the distribution of income and wealth, whereas measures such as a national minimum wage or a wealth tax would have a much more significant impact. Nevertheless, there can be some significant effects of public ownership on the distribution of income and wealth.

The effect on the distribution of wealth is likely to be negligible if the current shareholders are paid (in cash or in government bonds) the current stock market valuation. Indeed, in so far as existing shareholders are over-compensated, the immediate effect is to enhance the wealth of the shareholders. Although some shareholders are relatively wealthy individuals, much shareholding is by pension funds, etc (as discussed below in Chapter 5). Thus, although the precise impact on the distribution of wealth of taking a company into public ownership may be complex , it is unlikely to have any major immediate impact.

Another effect on the distribution of income comes from the pricing structure of utilities and other suppliers. The pricing structure of utilities generally involves a fixed charge for the right to have a supply and a variable charge depending on usage. The balance between the fixed charge and the variable charge impacts on the distribution of income. Since usage generally rises with income, a relatively high fixed charge and relatively low variable charges would benefit the more affluent at the expense of the less affluent: 'Whatever benefits competition delivers, lower income groups are likely to achieve at best a smaller share, and at worst pay higher prices. This is particularly worrying when other safety nets are simultaneously being weakened' (Waddams Price, 1997, p121).

It is often argued (by economists) that price should reflect the incremental cost of provision. Otherwise people will be encouraged to buy that which has a low price (relative to cost) and discouraged from buying that which has a high price (relative to cost). But, for utilities, the incremental cost is generally much below the average cost: the extreme example being that the incremental cost (to the railways) of an additional passenger on a train which is not full is close to zero. Thus the use of prices reflecting incremental costs is not viable, and the extent to which they are charged leads to losses (as prices are then below average costs). In those industries where there are significant overheads (fixed costs which do not vary with output) and joint costs (when costs are shared by two or more different production activities), it is rather arbitrary exactly how prices are linked with costs. How the overhead and joint costs are recovered is essentially arbitrary, though economists have sought to devise rules for their recovery. Where a utility faces competition in some areas but not others, the likelihood is that it charges relatively low prices in areas of competition and relatively high prices elsewhere.

A related aspect concerns 'cream skimming' or 'cherry picking', that is where a firm will supply services where it is profitable to do so, but not elsewhere. Often the profitable provision will be to the relatively affluent able to pay a high price, and the unprofitable to the less affluent not able to pay premium prices. Postal services to rural areas are more costly to provide than those to urban areas, and a private company, left to its own devices, is likely to either not provide services to remote rural areas or to charge much more. Under privatisation there is market segmentation:

> ... the process of focusing on the most lucrative markets and consequently the customer (a company or individual) who will spend most on the most profitable services ... Cherry picked areas and companies immediately reap cheaper services, higher reliability and security, powers to negotiate preferential treatment and greater innovation in new services. More worryingly low income households are being penalised in pricing regimes and are being helped to cut themselves off from electric-

ity, gas, water and telephone services which they cannot afford (Marvin, Graham and Guy, 1996, p5).

So far, the licenses permitting the utility companies to operate have included universal service obligations which can limit the extent of 'cherry picking'.

The final aspect of distribution arises from the degree of inequality of wages, salaries and other incomes within the enterprise. There can be little doubt that, following privatisation, the salaries of the 'top' managers in many privatised companies increased dramatically. UNISON (1996) reports that:

> the remuneration packages (more commonly known as pay and perks) of the chairman of the water companies, for example, have increased by 224 % since 1989, the last full year before privatisation. These packages include bonuses of up to £75,000, which are dependent on the performance of the company. In addition executive chairmen and other executive directors hold share options which, when exercised, can realise a small fortune (pp 37/38).

Table 1 provides some further examples.

Table 1
Changes in salaries of directors following privatisation

Company	Increase in directors' salaries after privatisation (%)
Amersham International	329 (3)
Associated British Ports	67 (2)
British Aerospace	181 (5)
BP	101 (5)
British Telecom	136 (3)
Britoil	36 (2)
Cable and Wireless	352 (3)
Enterprise Oil	215 (2)
National Freight Consortium	93 (2)
British Airways	242 (2)
British Gas	68 (2)

Note: The number in parenthesis indicates the number of years over which the reported change in salary occurred. For comparison, the average increase in earnings in the first half of the 1980s was 7.5 % per annum.
Source: Clarke (1993)

There has been a considerable and arbitrary redistribution of income and wealth in the process of privatisation, much of which would now be difficult to reverse. Besides the gains which accrue to many who bought into (under-priced) share issues on the flotation of privatised companies, there have been some spectacular gains for a few. As this is written, the most recent case is that of the rolling stock companies on the railways. British Rail's train leasing companies (Roscos) were sold for £700 million less than they were worth according to the National Audit Office (*Observer*, 8 March 1998).

We conclude this section by arguing that improving the distribution of income and wealth is unlikely to be a major objective of public ownership but that public ownership can be designed to have a favourable impact on the (effective) distribution of income. The pricing structure of the utilities can be designed to reflect distributional considerations in a way which is unlikely under regulation, given the pressures to maximise profits by the privatised utilities. In a similar vein, the wage and salary structure of a publicly owned utility is likely to involve less inequality than that of a privatised utility, and there is considerable historical evidence to support this view.

ENVIRONMENTAL CONSIDERATIONS

The industries which are at the forefront of debates over public ownership, namely electricity, gas and water, are also industries which raise many environmental concerns. These concerns are, of course, not unique to those industries but are particularly acute in them. It could be argued that whilst the environmental considerations are more acute, dealing with them raises no particular issues of principle. In other words, the general approach to environmental considerations can be applied to those industries as to any other. The general approach has been (in principle, if not in practice) to have a mixture of taxes on pollution or on the causes of pollution (e.g. the differential tax on leaded over unleaded petrol); subsidies (e.g. in areas of special scientific interest); and direct controls (e.g. emission standards). In the particular case of the water industry, environmental regulation is undertaken by the NRA (National Rivers Authority), which is now part of the Environment Agency set up in April 1996.

In the case of gas and electricity, the relevant effects arise largely from the environmental impact of the production and usage of the energy sources. The privatised companies are to some degree subject to price caps but are not limited in the amount which they produce and sell at the capped price. Thus the companies have incentives to produce and sell as much as possible (assuming that the capped price covers their unit costs, and indeed if costs fall with output there is some extra encouragement to increase volume), and have no incentives to promote energy conservation and efficiency.

The managers of a publicly owned utility may have some incentives to make their business as large as possible (and hence to promote production), but it would be possible to provide clear incentives for these managers to promote energy efficiency. Regulation of the privatised utilities could be used in a similar manner, e.g. to insist that a given proportion of sales revenue is used to promote energy conservation, but problems of monitoring and effectiveness arise. Taxation (such as a carbon tax or an energy tax) could be used, but whatever the merits of such taxation, it can be levied whether the industry is under private or public ownership, and clearly does not rely on the form of ownership involved. The potential difference which public ownership can make arises from the change in the organisation's objectives. A private company is run for profit, though it can be subject to regulation and it may find environmentally friendly policies to be profitable. A publicly owned company can be operated in pursuit of other objectives which, as we will argue below, need to be clearly specified and monitored to ensure accountability and compliance.

Cost of capital

The government can borrow at prime rates, reflecting its high credit rating: currently the rate of interest on government bonds (i.e. the rate at which the government can effectively borrow) is around 8 per cent. The effective rate at which the government can borrow is even lower: to the extent to which interest payments by the government are taxable, the appropriate cost to the government is the post-tax rate of interest. Further, the real cost of borrowing is diminished by the rate of inflation, though this is rarely reflected in the presentation of government accounts. Taking tax and inflation into account would mean that the government can currently borrow at a cost to the government of around 3 per cent per annum in real terms.

When making decisions on capital projects, the government often judges the estimated benefits from a proposed project against a test rate of return, which is currently 8 per cent. This is a real rate of return, and hence is significantly above the rate at which the government can borrow money but could be viewed as incorporating some allowance for risk and uncertainty.

The cost of capital for private companies is not a straightforward matter as companies can raise finance through a variety of channels (e.g. bank lending, issue of equity) which have different costs and different tax treatments. But what is relevant here is the rate of return required by the private sector and that required by the public sector. Hutton (1995, p151) reports, from a study by Coopers and Lybrand, that the over-all cost of capital, including debt service, dividend payments, shareholders' profit requirements and tax payments in Britain averaged over the period 1983-91 at 19.9 per cent (as compared with 14.7 per cent in Japan, 15.1 per cent in US and 15.7 per cent in Germany). Yet the public sector is still requiring a rate of return which is substantially above the rate at which it can borrow. Whatever the precise figures, it would seem to be the case that the required rate of return for the public sector is substantially below that required for the private sector.

Although the main form of regulation of privatised utilities has fallen on the so-called RPI – x formula, there has been an element of the imposition of a rate of return. For example, in the Monopolies and Mergers Commission (1997) report on BG PLC it is argued that a 7 per cent real pre-tax cost of capital should be applied to the operations of Transco, though British Gas disputed that figure and argued for a higher one. In the case of the water industry, the Monopolies and Mergers Commission (1995) argued for a somewhat lower cost of capital in the range of 5 to 6 per cent.

This difference between the public sector and the private sector has implications for the prices of firms in the two sectors and also for the PFI (Private Finance Initiative). This can be readily expressed in the following way. Suppose that a capital project costs A, and the required rate of return is r and the rate of depreciation is d: the price charged for the product of this project to yield the required rate of return would then have to be at least $(r + d)A/Q + w/l + m$, where Q is the amount produced, and w/l is the unit labour cost (wage divided by labour productivity) and m unit material cost. Thus the price depends on capital charges, labour costs and material costs.

The rate of return actually reported will obviously depend on many factors, including the degree of efficiency. But for the utilities, it will crucially depend on the price charged, which in turn is regulated (whether the utility is in public or private hands) and typically much below what the utility could charge if unrestricted. Comparing rates of return between private and public companies, especially in the utility sectors, tells us little about comparative performance. But the rate of return is significant for the costs of the product to the consumers. The arguments given above suggest that prices may well be lower under public ownership than under private ownership, simply because the required rate of return is substantially lower in the former case than in the latter.

Advocates of PFI have in effect to argue that, although *r* is higher for the private sector than for the public sector (and hence the cost of the project higher if undertaken by the private sector), other costs of the project are much lower for the private sector. Clearly, this lower cost could come about from a lower cost of the project *(A)*, lower wages *(w)*, higher labour productivity *(l)* or lower material costs *(m)*.

But this argument can be contrasted with the experience prior to the launch of the PFI:

> Until 1989, government practice in this respect was directed by the so-called Ryrie rules – named after Sir William Ryrie who chaired a committee in the early 1980s which considered the issue of private finance for nationalised industries. Under the Ryrie rules, the use of private finance would only be allowed if the efficiency gains thereby generated were sufficiently large to compensate for the higher cost of private finance, a condition which in practice was never met (Bladen-Hovell, 1997, pp202-3).

The PFI has been seen as a form of creeping privatisation with the private sector owning and operating capital assets from which goods and services are produced and sold to the public sector, replacing goods and services which would have been provided internally by the public sector. The PFI is also viewed as a way of reducing the PSBR through the provision of finance by the private sector. But this is a false view in that whilst the private sector may finance, say, the construction of a school, it charges the public sector a rent on the school over many years into the future. The public sector avoids the outlay of capital expenditure on the school in the present, only to incur renting or leasing costs of the school for many years to come. Further, a commitment to lease an asset over a number of years is not dissimilar to the purchase of the asset, and accountants would consider the leasing commitment over the life-time of the asset as a capital obligation. In effect, the public sector is permitted to engage in accounting practices which would be frowned upon in the private sector.

Helm (1994, pp29-30) indicates that shareholders in public utilities have done rather well with 'the returns to shareholders greatly exceed[ing] the cost of capital, and exceed[ing] those in other countries' utility sectors. Shareholders have, in particular, done much better than under rate-of-return regulation'. He also argues that 'there is little *positive* evidence to suggest – outside the telecommunications sector – that British utility consumers have fared better than those in other comparator countries [where often utilities have remained nationalised]'.

This would suggest that privatised utilities require a higher rate of return than would be the case under public ownership. In such a case, public ownership would provide lower costs through the requirement for a lower rate of return.

PUBLIC OWNERSHIP AS A MODE OF REGULATION

The utilities, or at least those parts of them which form the basic network, are natural monopolies, and as such it is widely recognised that they have to be subject to some form of specific regulation. All industries are subject to a variety of forms of regulation over standards, employment practices, etc, but here we are concerned with the specific regulation of the utilities. The basic rationale for regulation of natural monopolies is that whilst efficiency considerations dictate that there should be a monopoly position, that opens up the way for the monopolistic exploitation of the consumers. This exploitation can take various forms including high prices and poor quality of service. Regulation has also been seen as necessary to ensure a universal supply obligation at (broadly) uniform prices.

The utilities can be located under the general rubric of – in the words of the new Clause 4 of the Labour Party – 'where those undertakings essential to the common good are either owned by the public or accountable to them'. Public ownership is then clearly seen as an alternative to regulation in the case of utilities. The problems of the regulation of privatised utilities are fully discussed in Chapter 4, and we limit ourselves to some general observation here.

Regulation faces problems of information collection, monitoring, agency capture, as well as those of devising rules of regulation which do not generate perverse incentives. Regarding the first of those it can be noted that the British regulatory system runs on a much smaller scale (in terms of numbers employed) than the American system, and it may be questioned whether the British system is large enough for the effective regulation of the designated industries. Agency capture summarises the case where the regulatory agency acts more in the interests of the producers than of the consumers. The rate of return regulation in the United States is often seen as an example of perverse incentives (since it does not encourage lower costs which would merely lead to lower prices, and it encourages 'over investment') ; these considerations were a major factor behind the adoption of the RPI – *x* rule (price increases *x* per cent below the rate of inflation) in this country.

Public ownership can be viewed as an alternative form of regulation:

> In most of these countries [Western European and Japan] natural monopolies were usually dealt with through public enterprises, which, technically, were not 'regulated' whereas, in the US, they were the primary targets for regulation. This difference is, of course, in many ways more nominal than substantive, because government ministries and agencies supervising the public enterprises in these countries had to deal with the same kinds of problems as those the US regulators faced (Chang, 1997, p 705).

Public ownership does not remove the requirement for regulation but it does, in effect, remove one layer of bureaucracy. Under the present system, the government creates and instructs the regulatory agency (OFTEL, OFWAT etc), and that agency then regulates and monitors the privatised utilities. With public ownership, the monitoring and regulation of the utility is undertaken directly by government. It should be recognised that public ownership does not remove the need for regulation, it simply takes a rather different form. Under public ownership, there are still matters such as the level and structure of prices, the universal service obligation and levels of investment to be determined, as well as how far these should be decided by the government and imposed on the utility or determined by the utility in pursuance of the general guidelines and objectives laid down by government.

REGULATORY FAILURE

The general pattern in the regulated industries is that a company is given a licence to provide a particular range of goods or services, e.g. a regional electricity company is given a licence to distribute electricity over a particular geographical area. The key features of these licences are:

(i) the licence gives the right to provide a service subject to constraints on the price to be charged, on the level of service (the universal service provision) and on the quality of service. The licences do not, in general, specify any requirements on the level of investment (and hence on the future level and security of potential supply).
(ii) the major concern over the levels of prices and profits in the privatised utilities has to date been over them being too high. However, the regulators are charged with ensuring that there is a supply (of electricity, gas, etc) and hence that profits are sufficient to ensure that the incumbent company maintains supply. Thus there are clear limits to how far prices and profits can be lowered without supply being placed in jeopardy.
(iii) the licences are generally provided 'free of charge' and without competition (rail services being a partial exception). The company *in situ* at the time of privatisation has continued with the licence, despite the changes of ownership and control which have occurred in many cases. For example, the company which now distributes electricity in the South East (Central and South West Corporation of America) has achieved that position through the acquisition of SEEB, and the aims and objectives of the current owners may be quite different from those of the initial owners. A contrast can be drawn between the licences granted to the privatised utilities and those relating to the television franchises which have long been subject to a selection process and are now subject to a bidding process (subject to a quality threshold).

Regulation in its nature tends to involve constraints rather than creation of opportunities. Describing the position in the first three decades after the war, Chang has commented that:

> The most important difference between the US and other developed countries, however, was in their objectives of regulation. In Western Europe and Japan ... the regulatory regime [involving public ownership] was often shaped by 'developmental' objectives, which put emphasis on 'dynamic' considerations (such as improving productivity, upgrading technology, and achieving efficient structural change), whereas the US

> regulatory regime was mainly shaped by the concern for 'static' productive and allocative efficiencies, and some concern for equity' (Chang, 1997, p706).

The problems of regulation are considered in much more detail in Chapter 4. It suffices to say here that regulation of privatised utilities cannot ensure universal supply and adequate investment, and those utilities will only supply if it is perceived to be profitable to do so.

CONCLUSIONS

This chapter has explored many of the major arguments for public ownership, especially of the utilities. In the next two chapters we explore issues of the comparative performance of public enterprises and private enterprises, and the problems of regulating privatised utilities. In other chapters we will comment on ways of seeking to ensure that public ownership provides high quality and responsive services.

3

Comparative performance of public and private ownership

Introduction

This chapter discusses the performance of publicly owned enterprises in comparison with the performance of privately owned ones. Public enterprises are those which sell their output rather than those which provide services free at the point of use (e.g. the health service). The purpose of this review of the evidence on comparative performance is a simple one, namely to see if the argument often used against public ownership, that it is less efficient than private ownership, is valid. In Chapter 6 we discuss some of the theoretical arguments on the comparative performance of public ownership and private ownership, but in this chapter our concern is with the empirical evidence.

Making comparisons between the performance and efficiency of private and public sector companies is not a straightforward exercise for two basic reasons. First, a reasonable comparison should be made between companies which are in a broad sense comparable, though they must differ in terms of the key feature of the form of ownership. But public enterprises are more likely (than private enterprises) to be operating on a large scale, and to be involved in industries which are monopolistic or oligopolistic, and those structural features may affect corporate performance. Some public enterprises have been involved in industries which were generally in decline while other public enterprises have been in industries subject to rapid technological change, and those features will have an impact on the growth rate of productivity. These features of the environment within which a public or private enterprise operates will have a strong influence on their performance, and valid comparisons require that they are adequately taken into account.

There have usually been reasons why companies came into public ownership, often associated with perceptions of their failure in the private sector. The outstanding examples of this were British Leyland

and Rolls Royce in the 1970s, but many other nationalisations were in part stimulated by private sector failure. As Hannah (1994) observes: 'A common factor in early public ownership had been a perception by politicians of market failure, often buttressed by early cases of regulatory failure'. It is then possible that public enterprises appear to perform poorly because those enterprises have been taken into public ownership because they performed badly as private enterprises. It is also the case that poorly performing private enterprises are likely to go bankrupt and out of business, while poorly performing public enterprises may be able to remain in operation if any losses are underwritten by the government.

Second, comparisons between public sector companies and private sector ones are complicated by differences in the objectives of the two types of company. In the past public enterprises have been required to hold down prices to contribute to counter-inflationary policies, to maintain unprofitable services, and have been encouraged to maintain employment etc. The imposition of these objectives on public enterprise would clearly have an impact on many measures of performance such as productivity or profitability. It has also generally been the case that the range of activities which a public enterprise could undertake was severely limited : for example, British Rail was largely restricted to operating a railway service and was not permitted to diversify into other forms of transport. In this manner, public enterprises could not diversify away from relatively unprofitable activities into more profitable ones whereas private enterprises would be under no such limitations.

COMPARATIVE PERFORMANCE OF PUBLIC AND PRIVATE OWNERSHIP

The comparisons of performance of public enterprise with private enterprise have focused on measures such as productivity, level of costs and some measures of efficiency. The comparative profitability of public and private ownership is not a particularly useful measure to look at. Profitability is very much affected by the price obtained by the enterprise for its output, and public enterprises have in particular been subject to a regime of price control. The nationalised industries established by the Attlee government were, for example, instructed to break even on average, and later nationalised industries were given financial targets, and the profit record would be much affected by such instructions and targets.

The comparative efficiency of public and private enterprises is of much more interest than profitability. As further discussed in Chapter 6, efficiency refers to the relationship between inputs and output: how well inputs are used, and whether or not output is produced using as few inputs as technically possible.

Millward and Parker (1983) conducted a wide-ranging survey of the available evidence, and indicate the extensive difficulties in making comparisons between privately owned and publicly owned firms. They first survey some American studies which compare companies in the electricity industry where public and private firms co-exist. They conclude that 'none of the cost studies support the proposition that public electricity firms have a lower productivity or higher unit costs than private firms, allowing for differences in output and in factor prices though one qualification may be mentioned ... [the] possibility that public firms have a lower cost of capital' (p244). They also noted that 'the major conclusion that can be drawn from the case of Australian airlines is similar to that for Canadian railways – there is no significant evidence that productivity is lower in public firms than private firms' (p239).

Their overall assessment of a large number of studies is that:

> Whilst the results are rather mixed, there is some evidence that competition does reduce the costs of public firms and regulation raises the costs of private firms. Neither finding is inconsistent with the findings about the effects of 'ownership' on costs – namely that, balancing the results of electricity and railroads against water, airlines and refuse collection, there is no general indication that private firms are more cost efficient than public firms (p251).

Ferguson (1988) summarised 15 comparisons of public and private sector efficiency. Eight of these refer to American electricity generation with the following conclusions: two studies report no difference between the sectors, three report the public enterprise as more efficient and one reports private firms as more efficient. One study finds both types of firm with costs 2.5 % above the competitive level, and the final study reports that private firms sell wholesale electricity at higher prices and buy in at lower prices (than public sector firms). The results of the other seven studies (covering water, rail and airlines) are similar in tone.

In a similar vein, Yarrow (1986) concludes his own survey by saying that:

> Private sector monitoring [i.e. private ownership] is more efficient where the relevant firm faces strong competition and other forms of product and factor market failure are relatively unimportant ... The evidence on comparative performance in cases where product and factor market inefficiencies are substantive is much less clear cut. Indeed, in examples such as electricity supply it tends to point in the other direction, towards better performance by public firms.

The effects of nationalisation

In this section, we review some studies which have made comparisons between the performance of the British nationalised industries as a group and the performance of some other industries. The previous section made comparisons between individual companies, and the purpose of this section is the same, namely to investigate whether there is any systematic difference in performance between publicly owned and privately owned companies.

Tables 3.1 and 3.2 provide some data on the comparative productivity performance of nationalised industries in the UK. Given what has

Table 3.1

Comparative performance of UK public enterprises and manufacturing sector (average annual growth rates in per cent)

	1951-64	1964-73	1973-85
Public enterprises			
Labour	-0.6	-2.3	-1.2
Labour productivity	3.3	5.0	2.1
Capital	2.3	2.8	0.7
Capital productivity	0.4	0.1	0.2
Total factor productivity	2.4	2.9	1.4
Manufacturing			
Labour	0.7	-1.1	-3.1
Labour productivity	2.5	4.0	2.3
Capital	4.0	3.6	1.4
Capital productivity	-0.8	-0.7	-2.2
Total factor productivity	1.9	2.4	1.1

Source: Millward (1991)

Table 3.2

Productivity growth rates in core nationalised industries and manufacturing

Labour productivity growth

	1948-58	1958-68	1968-78	1978-85
Steel	n.a.	n.a.	-0.2	12.6
Airlines	14.0	8.9	6.4	6.6
Electricity	4.6	8.0	5.3	3.9
Gas	1.6	5.5	8.5	3.8
Road Freight	0.8	4.9	n.a.	n.a.
Coal	0.9	4.7	-0.7	4.4
Railways	0.6	4.3	0.8	3.9
Buses	-0.6	-1.4	-0.5	2.1
Post Office	n.a.	n.a.	-1.3	2.3
Telecommunications	n.a.	n.a.	8.2	5.8
Total manufacturing	1.9	3.7	2.7	3.0

Total factor productivity growth

	1948-58	1958-69	1968-78	1979-88
Steel	n.a.	n.a.	2.5	12.9
Airways	7.8	9.1	5.5	n.a.
Electricity	3.6	3.1	0.7	1.4
Gas	0.7	3.7	n.a.	3.3
Coal	0.4	3.0	-1.4	2.9
Rail	n.a.	2.4	-1.4	1.3
Post Office	n.a.	n.a.	n.a.	3.7
Telecommunications	n.a.	n.a.	n.a.	2.4
Airports	n.a.	n.a.	n.a.	1.6
Manufacturing	1.5	2.4	1.7	2.6

n.a. = not available or not appropriate

Notes: For steel, airlines and telecommunications, slightly different dates apply. Manufacturing includes some publicly owned companies, particularly in the 1970s.

Source: Hannah (1994, Tables 6.5)

been said above, it will be realised that finding a suitable comparison for the nationalised industries is difficult, and the authors on whose work these tables draw have made the comparison with manufacturing industry. The growth rate of productivity varies considerably across industries, and it would generally be expected that the growth rate would be lower in the service industries than in the production industries. Manufacturing industry was, of course, mainly privately owned whereas many public enterprises operated in the utilities or transport, and the underlying rate of technological change may be quite different in manufacturing as compared with the utilities and transport. Thus manufacturing industry may not be the most suitable comparison to use, if the technological conditions there are significantly different from those in the industries in which public enterprises have operated. It should also be noted that calculations of productivity growth can be sensitive to the choice of start and end dates: productivity is often relatively high as output is high during a boom, and relatively low in recession. Two productivity measures are deployed. The first is labour productivity, and the second total factor productivity. The first has the shortcoming that labour productivity may increase because large amounts of capital are being poured into an industry (a criticism which has sometimes been made of the nationalised industries). To make allowance for the effects of investment in capital equipment, total factor productivity is output divided by a weighted sum of labour and capital inputs.

From these tables, it can first be seen that public enterprises were shedding labour throughout the period covered, as was manufacturing, apart from the earlier period of 1951-64. The capital stock in the public enterprises tended to grow more slowly than for manufacturing as a whole. It can be seen that whereas for the manufacturing sector capital productivity (that is output divided by capital stock) declined, it rose – albeit at a very slow pace – in the public enterprises. The growth of labour productivity was faster in the public enterprises than in manufacturing for the two earlier periods of 1951-64 and 1964-73 and virtually the same in the period of 1973-85. The growth of total factor productivity was faster in the public enterprises than in manufacturing in each of the three periods considered.

Table 3.2 indicates a wide range of experience on the growth of labour productivity and of total factor productivity across the nationalised industries. This is a reminder of the influence of a wide range of factors on productivity growth other than the form of ownership, and in particular the influence of technological change and the buoyancy of demand facing an industry.

One author has then concluded that:

> The UK public enterprise sector therefore does not have an inferior productivity growth record to that of private manufacturing. How does

> it compare internationally over time ? ... Three points emerge. First is that over the whole post-war period, comparative sector productivity in the British and American economies has been stable ... [The public utilities] as a group [in the UK] had an inferior relative output per head before nationalisation. Second it is clear that whilst the comparative labour productivity of manufacturing has not changed (nor that of agriculture and construction significantly) the UK public enterprise sector has advanced over the post-war period relative to the US industries in the same product area. US output per head for the broad group of extractive industries and utilities declined, taking UK = 100, from 769 in 1950, to 517 in 1968, to 323 in 1977. Transport declined from 458 to 240 to 213 and within that total railways and airlines have clearly been part of the UK improvement in relative labour productivity ... The third point is that some of the improvements are of course simply structural – the rise in UK oil exploration in the 1970s clearly affecting the UK figure for extractive industries – whilst in certain cases (coal, communications) the British performance, in labour productivity at least, has worsened relative to US (Millward, 1991, pp145-6).

Making comparisons of similar industries between countries can also be useful in that it may be assumed that the technological opportunities facing the same industry in different countries are broadly similar. The figures in Table 3.3. make comparisons between labour productivity in UK industries where enterprises were largely publicly owned with the same industries in the United States and Germany. In the USA these industries are largely privately owned, although as noted above there are some publicly owned electricity companies and, as will be mentioned in Chapter 7, there are mutual organisations in the utilities. In Germany these industries are largely publicly owned. It can be seen that labour productivity in these industries is much higher in the other two countries, particularly in the United States. But the differences in productivity in these industries are on a par with the differences in productivity in the manufacturing industries which are largely privately owned in all three countries.

Table 3.4 provides some comparisons between the UK and the USA in terms of total factor productivity growth over the period 1950 to 1985, and sub periods. It can be seen that in manufacturing the growth rates are very close, and indeed for the whole period of 1950-85 the same. In mining, productivity grew faster in the publicly owned British coal industry than in the privately owned American industry. In gas, electricity and water, the British performance was better overall, and notably so in the period 1966 to 1973. The picture is mixed in transport and communications, where the range of figures for the USA refers to the component parts.

Table 3.3 Comparative labour productivity in 1970-5

	West Germany/UK	USA/UK
Gas 1975	2.21	3.32
Electricity 1975	2.11	3.54
Water 1975	0.99	1.97
Railway 1970	1.08	3.95
Local bus/rail 1970	1.34	1.45
Post and telecommunications	1.08	2.28-3.17

For all manufacturing industries, the productivity gap was given on a year-by-year basis and over the period 1968 to 1977 the estimated West Germany/UK productivity gap varied from 1.31 to 1.52 and the USA/UK gap from 2.68 to 2.94.

Source: Hannah (1994) put together the table, the productivity gaps were originally estimated by Smith, Hitchens and Davies (1982).

These comparisons of productivity growth between industries and between countries do not support any superiority of private ownership over public ownership.

Table 3.4 Average annual growth of total factor productivity 1950-85

	1950-65	1966-73	1973-85	1950-85
Manufacturing				
UK	1.9	2.4	1.3	1.8
USA	2.0	1.8	1.4	1.8
Mining				
UK	1.5	2.2	-1.0	0.9
USA	0.5	1.9	-4.3	-0.6
Gas, electricity and water				
UK	3.3	4.3	1.8	3.1
USA	3.7	2.4	1.2	2.6
Transport and communications				
UK	2.4	3.7	2.3	2.5
USA	1.0-2.7	1.6-3.0	0.1-2.3	0.9-2.6

Source: Millward (1991, p. 147): the precise periods used vary slightly for UK and for USA

THE EFFECTS OF PRIVATISATION

The British experience of privatisation has now also provided evidence of the relative efficiency of the public and private sectors. Privatisation has involved more than a change of ownership, namely in a range of cases vertical disintegration and the relatively recent introduction of competition (notably in gas and electricity supply). Hence distinguishing the precise effects of a change from public to private ownership may be problematic. The studies on which we draw here do not use data which extend past 1992, and the studies are concerned with the privatisation which took place during the 1980s.

In many cases, the proposals for privatisation were known some years before it actually occurred: or at least many thought they knew which industries were on the agenda for privatisation. There were also some notable delays in the privatisation programme. In some cases, there was extensive restructuring of the firm which in the government's view prepared the firm for privatisation: British Airways is perhaps the best known example. The restructuring, which often involved substantial reductions in employment, had impacts prior to privatisation.

Parker and Martin (1995) studied eleven firms transferred from the public sector to the private sector in the 1980s. These firms were British Gas, British Steel Corporation, British Telecom, the National Freight Corporation, British Airways, British Aerospace, Jaguar Cars, Rolls Royce, Britoil, the British Airports Authority and Associated British Ports. The effects of privatisation are measured in terms of labour productivity and total factor productivity. The changes in productivity were measured for five distinct periods:

(i) nationalisation;
(ii) pre-privatisation;
(iii) post-announcement of privatisation;
(iv) post-privatisation period;
(v) the 1989-92 recession.

Each of the periods generally covered four years. The nationalisation period varied between firms but was generally some period from the late 1970s into the early 1980s, and hence generally covered the recession of the early 1980s. It is also the case that the overall rate of productivity growth in the economy was faster in the 1980s than in the 1970s. The productivity growth in the nationalisation period may then

Table 3. 5 Productivity pre- and post-privatisation

Annual percentage change in labour productivity

	National-isation period	Pre-privatisation period	Post announce-ment period	Post privatisation period	Recession period
British Airways	6.6	10.8	8.6	2.9	4.8
British Airports Authority (1)	2.3	2.6	1.4	-1.4	-4.7
British Airports Authority (2)	1.2	5.9	5.1	2.3	-2.1
Britoil	-1.2	2.7	9.3	6.3	n.a.
British Gas	2.4	6.8	5.8	3.7	1.6
British Steel	25.4	11.3	13.9	-0.9	-0.4
British Aerospace	0.6	0.6	3.3	6.3	-14.4
Jaguar	34.9	27.0	3.6	3.7	-15.7
Rolls Royce	7.4	6.5	4.0	1.6	4.2
National Freight	0.3	5.7	11.4	4.4	0.4
Associated British Ports	-3.4	3.0	9.3	15.4	24.1
British Telecom	6.8	6.9	6.9	7.3	8.3

Annual percentage change in total factor productivity

	National-isation period	Pre-privatisation period	Post announce-ment period	Post privatisation period	Recession period
British Airways	2.4	4.9	1.4	6.7	5.3
British Airports Authority (1)	1.9	-0.8	-2.2	-7.6	-5.9
British Airports Authority (2)	1.1	2.5	1.3	-4.3	-3.6
Britoil	15.3	13.4	9.7	9.6	n.a.
British Gas	0.7	1.4	2.7	-2.1	0.2
British Steel	11.7	4.5	7.5	-4.4	-4.0
British Aerospace	-2.1	-2.1	-4.1	-0.2	-1.0
Jaguar	9.1	6.1	-1.4	0.7	-14.9
Rolls Royce	-0.3	5.0	-2.4	0.5	-0.6
National Freight	-0.2	-0.9	-0.3	4.1	-2.1
Associated British Ports	2.8	6.9	12.2	11.4	5.0
British Telecom	11.0	4.0	2.9	5.8	5.2

Note: Alternative estimates are made for British Airports Authority.
Source: Martin and Parker (1995)

be depressed in so far as that period covers the recession of the early 1980s and/or the late 1970s.

Some of their results are summarised in Table 3.5. The pattern is clearly mixed. There are some spectacular changes, with slumps in the performance of Jaguar and British Steel after privatisation but improvements in the case of Associated British Ports. It can be seen that there are cases of productivity improvement with privatisation, and cases of deterioration.

Boussofiane, Martin and Parker (1997) consider a similar sample of companies except that Britoil and British Telecom are omitted. They begin by remarking that:

> Research into the actual effects of privatization, however, has produced mixed results. In some cases productivity growth does not seem to have increased significantly after privatization. Where there have been noticeable efficiency gains, these have tended to occur mainly in the run-up to privatization, where the industries were rationalised and prepared for sale, suggesting 'one-off' efficiency improvements (p297).

Their own work leads them to conclude that:

> The basic DEA [data envelopment analysis: the technique of analysis which they use] model suggests that privatization has been associated with an improvement in efficiency at British Airways, ABP and British Gas. There also appears to have been an anticipation effect, in the sense that there is evidence that performance improved at British Airways, British Airports Authority and British Steel in the two or three years before privatization. However, for British Airports Authority and British Steel this efficiency improvement was not sustained through to the end of the sample period. For British Aerospace, NFC and Rolls-Royce, there is no obvious relationship between ownership and efficiency in these results. Thus although there is evidence of clear efficiency improvements in some cases, for other organizations there is little discernible difference between pre- and post-privatization performance (p309).

CONCLUSIONS

This chapter has reviewed the evidence pertaining to the comparative performance of publicly owned corporations versus privately owned corporations. Previous surveys have generally concluded that there is no systematic difference, and in particular that perceptions of inferior performance by publicly owned corporations are not sustained. However these surveys have generally concluded that competition has an effect on comparative performance. This chapter has also reported on the positive effects of previous nationalisations on performance, and the review of the impact of privatisation on performance presents a rather mixed picture. It could also be said that on the traditional performance criteria, there are considerable variations within public enterprises (as there would be within private enterprises).

4

ISSUES OF REGULATION

INTRODUCTION

The alternative to public ownership of the utilities is the continuation of private ownership with a combination of regulation and competition. It is generally recognised that the natural monopoly elements of the utilities will require continuing regulation. In those areas, such as gas and electricity supply, where competition has been introduced, there will need to be continuing regulation over access to the basic network. There will also be a need for a system of licensing for those who are permitted to supply gas and electricity on the grounds of safety and compatibility with the distribution network. It is also likely that there will be continuing regulation of charges made by the network for access to it.

The issues of regulation have spawned a considerable literature on the technicalities of regulation, and have also generated significant employment for economic consultants advising the parties involved. In this chapter we focus our attention on the more general issues raised by regulation, and point to its problematic nature.

Our discussion of the issues of regulation begins with the problem of ensuring that the regulatory agency operates to achieve policy objectives. In the American literature this has been much discussed under the heading of 'agency capture', meaning that the regulated firms come to have substantial influence over the regulatory agency, with the agency acting more in the interests of the producers than of the consumers. This is followed by a section on problems of information and implementation of regulation. It can be noted that the regulatory bodies in the UK have operated on a much smaller scale than those in the USA. The next section considers different modes of regulation: for example formulae such as RPI – x (where RPI is the rate of inflation, and hence utility prices are constrained to rise below the rate of inflation) have been used in the UK, whereas rate of return regulation has generally been used in the USA. The latter was said to have perverse incentives which the British formula was designed to avoid. But the setting of *x* has been problematic, and the windfall tax on public utilities has been a recognition of the high level of profits (and management salaries) which have resulted from this form of regulation and the way in which the industries were privatised. We then briefly consider the relationship between competition and regulation, before turning to some remarks on the recent Green Paper (Cmnd 3898: *Modernising the Framework for Utility Regulation*) and proposals for changes to the regulatory framework.

AGENCY CAPTURE

The effectiveness of any system of regulation is heavily dependent upon the regulators, not only in terms of their competence and the information available to them, but also in terms of the objectives and interests which they pursue. The argument has been made, particularly by American critics of regulation, that there will be a degree of 'agency capture' by the utility (its owners and mangers) of the regulatory agency (for example Stigler, 1971; for a critique of that approach see Tomlinson, 1993). The general thrust of this argument is that the regulatory agency will come to reflect the interests of the producers (private utility) rather than the consumers. 'The danger is that the regulatory authority, far from controlling and diminishing the monopoly power of the regulated firm, instead becomes the firm's advocate, and may be even an instrument for the maintenance of monopoly power by preventing new entry' (Rees and Vickers, 1995, p366). The number of producers is very small (often one firm) whereas there are numerous consumers. The effects of regulation are likely to be negative as far as the producer is concerned (e.g. profits may be restricted), but concentrated on the few (perhaps one) firms involved. In contrast, the effects for consumers may well be beneficial, but the benefits are spread over millions of consumers. The benefits for any individual consumer can be relatively small even when the aggregate benefits are substantial. Thus the producer has a strong incentive to seek favourable treatment by the regulatory agency. An individual consumer is unlikely to find it worthwhile to lobby the regulatory agency since lobbying involves costs whereas the (incremental) benefits to the individual are likely to be small.

Personal contact and interchange of personnel between regulatory agency and regulated firm can lead the agency to act in the interests of the firm it is formally charged to regulate. Those employed by the regulatory agency will require knowledge of the industry which is being regulated. This often means that there will be an interchange of staff between the regulatory agency and the regulated firms. In particular, those with knowledge of the workings of the regulatory agency and the industry may well be hired by the regulated firms on account of that expertise. The numbers employed by the regulatory agency may be small relative to the numbers employed by the company being regulated and the latter may be able to engulf the former with (perhaps irrelevant) information.

There is a sense in which the government has recognised a form of agency capture or at least that the regulatory system worked in the interests of the owners of the regulated companies. In commenting on the Green Paper, Margaret Beckett said that 'for too long, householders ... have felt that shareholders' interests have come first ... For the first time, the consumer interest will be put at the heart of the regulatory system' (DTI Press Release, 25 March 1998). Others have argued that agency capture has so far been muted:

> At first sight RPI – x regulation, and the British regulatory institutional structure more generally, may appear to have little vulnerability to capture, because the business of checking that annual price increases comply with the formula involves little regulatory discretion. However, regulators have had a good deal of discretion with RPI – x regulation in practice, and the regulatory process in Britain is not open to public scrutiny – the regulator does not have to explain or justify his decisions or publish the evidence on which they were based. Nevertheless ... there is little evidence so far that regulatory bodies have been subject to capture since privatisation (Rees and Vickers, 1995, pp366-7).

Any regulatory body is subject to a wide range of influences on its deliberations. But it is plausible to think, in the case of bodies regulating utilities, that lobbying and influence by the regulated companies may well have much more impact than that of workers, consumers or potential entrants into the industry. At a minimum, we can say that there is the ever present danger that regulation will come to operate mostly in the interests of the regulated.

INFORMATION AND IMPLEMENTATION

One of the problems raised in connection with any form of regulation is whether or not the government or its agents (in this case the regulatory agency) has the information needed to make correct decisions and then the information needed to ensure that decisions are implemented.

In the case of the utilities, the information needed for decision making would include costs and potential for cost reductions, innovation and investment and, for implementation, accurate information on profits, prices and costs. This is sometimes referred to in the literature as the problem of asymmetric information (as in some of the quotes below). The problem of asymmetric information is simply that one person or group of people involved have much more information than the other person or group of people. In the context of regulation, the regulated firm or industry generally has much more information on its own costs, possibilities for cost reduction and innovation, etc. than the regulator can have. The regulated firm will have incentives to withhold information from the regulator and incentives to provide only favourable information.

Before discussing some of the issues on information, it can be noted that British regulatory agencies operate with a relatively small number of staff. For example, OFFER has around 200 and OFTEL has around 150. It is generally acknowledged that the American regulatory system (which is state rather than federal based) operates on a much greater scale (after allowance for differences in size of population).

Problems of information are partially recognised in the recent Green Paper which talks of price adjustments 'when they [the utility companies] have deliberately misled the regulator by providing incomplete or inaccurate information when the price cap was set'. The dispute between British Gas and the regulator in 1987 when British Gas initially refused to supply sufficient information to enable a judgement to be made on the forecasts of prices was an early example of the difficulties of securing information. An example of inadequate or misleading information is the circumstances which came to light during the take-over bid by Trafalgar House for Northern Electric, whose second defence document indicated that the company would make payments of over £5 per share to its shareholders, in part financed by a substantial increase in gearing. The document also commented on future operating costs and capital expenditure which suggested that costs were lower than indicated by the data which had been used by the regulator.

The evolving structure of the companies subject to regulation is raising difficulties for regulation in two ways. The first is that one source of information can be generated by so-called bench-mark competition. This simply means using the performance of one company (in terms of costs, prices, profits, innovation, etc) as a benchmark of what can be achieved, and then expecting a comparable performance from other companies which were previously not performing as well. The wave of take-overs amongst utilities (and a significant number have been blocked) has reduced the potential for such comparisons. Indeed the regulators have objected to some of the proposed mergers amongst utilities on precisely these grounds: 'Any reduction in the number of independent water (and sewerage) companies affects the Director's ability to compare their performance. The emergence of multi-utilities raises particular regulatory issues. Ofwat needs to be confident that customers do not pay too much for services provided by associated companies' (Ofwat, 1997).

The second is the diversified nature of the utility-based companies. In some cases, the diversification has arisen through take-overs between utility companies. One response to the regulatory issues raised by the links between gas and electricity companies may be to merge the regulators of the gas and the electricity industry, as proposed in the Green Paper on Regulation. But other forms of take-overs and diversification, whether involving firms within the same industry or across a range of industries, cannot be dealt with by a change in the structure of regulation. The essential difficulty which arises is that of ensuring the clear separation of the accounts and the activities of the regulated part of a company from those of the unregulated part. These problems have been summarised in the following way.

> Some of the most controversial problems in regulating multiproduct firms have to do with 'cost allocation' and determining when there is cross-subsidy between activities. Consider, for example, the problem of 'allocating costs' between telephone-call charges and exchange-line rentals, or between the activities of a firm that is regulated in some of its activities but not in others. Clearly it is in the interests of the regulated firm to allocate, however spuriously, as many joint costs as possible to its regulated activities ... Disputes about cost allocation, which are likely to be all the greater if information asymmetries are large, are a good illustration of the 'burden of regulation'. This point leads to questions about policy towards structure: should a regulated firm be allowed to diversify into other unregulated activities? If diversification worsens the regulator's asymmetric information problem ... then it may hamper the effectiveness of regulation – to the benefit of the firm and to the detriment of welfare. This suggests that regulatory policy should be prepared

to place some constraints on diversification by regulated firms (Rees and Vickers, 1995, p369).

A final issue is the question of what it is that is being regulated. The perception is that it is Water Company X or Regional Electricity Company Y which is being regulated, and in one sense that is correct. But in another it may not be: it is the service for which X or Y is licensed that is subject to regulation, no matter who actually provides that service. Hence, even if X or Y sub-contracts a service to another company, X or Y is still responsible to the regulator for that service.

This brief discussion illustrates some of the informational difficulties confronting effective regulation. The suggestion here would be that these informational difficulties will tend to increase as utilities diversify and make acquisitions. They would also tend to increase if regulation becomes more concerned with quality of service rather than with price and profits. It may also suggest that the burden of regulation on companies and on the regulatory agencies will tend to increase, and that effective regulation may require much larger regulatory agencies than is currently the case.

MODES OF REGULATION

The rationale for the regulation of 'natural monopolies' arises from their monopoly power, and hence focuses on control of their prices and/or profits. The direct route would appear to be to impose controls on the level of profits or the rate of profits, and indeed that has been the mode of regulation generally used with public utilities in the United States under the heading of rate of return regulation (hereafter ROR). In effect, public utilities there are constrained to a maximum rate of return on assets. This mode of regulation was rejected as a model for the UK as it was seen to have some undesirable effects. The basis of the argument was that a constraint on the rate of return provided the managers of public utilities with the wrong incentives. Consider what could happen when a company which had the potential to gain a high rate of return is constrained to report a lower rate of return (and that indeed would be the purpose of ROR regulation). Such a firm would have incentives to inflate costs (thereby reducing profits) and to increase the size of the assets (thereby allowing more profits in total to be earned from a larger asset base) in order for the reported rate of profit to be brought down to that required by the regulator. The regulator is also faced with the problem of determining which assets should be included in the asset base and at what valuation. This problem is particularly highlighted in the case of nuclear power plants which have often turned out to be much more expensive to operate than originally envisaged, and where the economic value of the nuclear power plant may be small or negative in the light of the costs of de-commissioning. The inflation of costs can arise from, inter alia, paying higher wages and salaries (including those of the managers themselves) and allowing productive inefficiencies to grow.

It should, though, be noted that rate of return regulation, through encouragement of the asset base, stimulates investment, and investment boosts capacity. This provides electricity companies with a greater ability to meet the peaks of demand, and to expand capacity ahead of demand.

> The justification for ROR [rate of return] regulation is couched largely in terms of allocative efficiency [that is limiting the high prices and low output in an industry] but its implementation may induce other inefficiencies. For example, it may encourage accounting practices that overstate capital valuations and thus mislead investors. Another drawback is that it requires substantial information about costs and demand to be made available to the regulator. This could induce bureaucratic inefficiencies and may lead to revelation problems. An issue that arises under ROR regulation is rate base selection, what is an appropriate choice for s (the rate of return constraint)? For these and other reasons there has been a shift towards less informationally demanding regulation through what is termed price cap regulatory mechanisms (Doyle, 1993).

The approach to utility regulation in Britain has been described as drawing on three principles: 'the rejection of rate-of-return regulation; the rejection of direct government control; and the rejection of the assumption of monopoly as a permanent feature' (Helm, 1994). The second principle led to the appointment of regulators who, subject to general specified duties, operate independently of government. The third principle is further discussed below.

The first principle leads to a general mode of regulation, the precise application of which varies between industries, generally described as 'RPI–x', where RPI refers to the general rate of inflation and x is a figure fixed by the relevant regulatory authority, presumably designed to reflect the productivity potential of the industry concerned relative to that of the wider economy. For example, productivity growth potential is generally viewed as high in the telecommunications industry through the implementation of new technologies.

The RPI–*x* rule was advocated in the Littlechild Report (Littlechild, 1983) where it was claimed that price capping regulation (PC) 'dominated ROR regulation in terms of restraining monopoly power, promoting competition, reducing X-inefficiency and by providing incentives for cost reductions' (Doyle, 1993). In this quote, X-inefficiency can be read as including payments to managers and workers higher than necessary as well as technical inefficiency.

The RPI–*x* approach suffers from a number of difficulties. The idea behind this approach is that any gains from costs rising more slowly than prices (which rise at RPI–*x*) are retained by the regulated company to provide incentives for the companies to reduce costs. But there is a ratchet effect in operation whereby the achieved cost reductions and productivity growth in one period feed into the target cost reductions and productivity growth for the next period. Information on productivity growth potential is difficult (or perhaps impossible) to acquire, though past performance and that achieved in other countries may provide some guide. If the regulator underestimates the productivity growth potential, then there can be a profit bonanza for the utility concerned. But if that underestimated potential is achieved (wholly or partly) then the utility may suffer in subsequent periods through the value of *x* in the formula being raised, and hence providing some incentive for the utility to not fully achieve its potential. There is no explicit consideration of quality, and there would be some incentive for the regulated firm to lower quality which would reduce its costs though it may be able to obtain the same (capped) price for the product. This has led to the use of other mechanisms to check on quality such as levels of services agreements.

Although the emphasis has been on the use of the RPI–*x* rule, there are also significant rate of return considerations. 'The importance of return calculations in price reviews should be emphasised. The implicit use of rate-of-return in price reviews, and in setting *X* at the time of privatisation, has been widely acknowledged' (Rees and Vickers, 1995, p380). The authors continue by mentioning a number of instances in which cost of capital estimates have been used, generally in the range 5 to 8 per cent. It is perhaps not surprising that the regulated companies have argued for a higher rate of return than the regulator (which can include the Monopolies and Mergers Commission). The regulators have generally argued that the regulated companies are involved in a low risk business, and hence should accept a rate of return which is lower than the average elsewhere in the economy.

The significance of this is twofold. First, it illustrates that in practice there has been a mixture of regulation based on RPI–x with rate of return regulation. Although the Green Paper indicates the continuation of the RPI–x approach, this is modified by a mention of recouping 'unearned benefits'. Second, in effect the regulated utilities have to be guaranteed a minimum rate of return: otherwise they will be reluctant to undertake new investment and may consider withdrawal or at least a run down of their operations.

REGULATION AND COMPETITION

Some involved with regulation have seen it as a temporary measure, until competition has evolved from the monopoly positions given to the privatised utilities. An early reflection of this is: 'competition is by far the most effective means of protection against monopoly. Vigilance against anti-competitive practices is also important. Profit regulation is merely a "stop-gap" until sufficient competition develops' (Littlechild, 1983, p1).

The rationale for the regulation of the utilities has generally been the absence of competition, both actual and potential. There are two features of privatisation and the subsequent regulation which are relevant here. The first is that in some public utilities the industry has not been privatised as a single unit but rather has been vertically disintegrated. The two clearest examples of this are: the separation of the electricity industry into transmission (the National Grid), electricity production (PowerGen and National Power plus Nuclear Electric) and distribution and supply (twelve regional electricity companies); and the privatisation of the railways into RailTrack (responsible for the track) and regional train companies. The significance of this vertical disintegration is that whilst some parts of the industry are subject to decreasing costs (e.g. the national distribution of electricity), others may not be (e.g. the economies of scale in electricity generation are exhausted at a level of output which is a small proportion of total demand). Thus a natural monopoly may remain in some parts but not in others.

The second feature is the introduction of competition into many of the regulated industries, albeit that the competition has been under the scrutiny of the regulator. Of the privatised utilities, it is only the water industry where there has not been some entry of new competitors.

It is only recently that there has been much change in the extent of competition in the utilities. There has been some competition in electricity generation between PowerGen and National Power, albeit competition between two dominant producers in a situation of duopoly. Competition in the supply of gas and of electricity is now being introduced across the country. Some have seen this as the beginning of regulation through competition and of the withering away of regulation.

It is likely that regulation in some form will remain over both gas and electricity supply even though competition has been introduced. The regulation over prices and profits may decline, but there will be a remaining need for regulation over the quality of supply (for safety reasons), over the structure of prices and on universal supply obligations (or at least some notion of residual supplier). Some of this is recognised in the Green Paper which indicates that 'the energy regulators, with the energy companies, should develop an action plan to ensure that disadvantaged consumers benefit from improved efficiency, more choice and greater fairness'.

The perception of a requirement for continuing regulation over prices and profits depends on views of how competition will evolve in the supply of gas and electricity. It could be expected that initially there will be a substantial number of firms offering gas or electricity supply (or often both) but that there will be a shake-out leaving a few dominant firms. Those firms which are successfully established will enjoy advantages over potential entrants into gas or electricity supply. The established firms will have customers signed up for some time ahead and will have billing and other networks in place, which will put any new entrants at a significant disadvantage. It could then be expected that a relatively small number of dominant gas and electricity suppliers will emerge with significant market power.

PROPOSALS FOR CHANGE

The Green Paper on Utility Regulation (Cmnd. 3898 : Modernising the Framework for Utility Regulation) does not propose any fundamental change to the present system of regulation. It should be noted that it covers gas, electricity, water and telecommunications but not the railways. A structural change is proposed to integrate the regulation of the gas and electricity industries, and this is a reflection of the mergers amongst energy companies, which have made the separation of gas and electricity operations increasingly difficult. There are intentions that more regard should be given to consumers' interests, though it is unclear what that would amount to in practice. It is proposed that 'the framework for economic regulation set out in the duties and functions of the regulators needs to enable a balance to be set between consumers and shareholders which delivers fair and efficient results for both'. It is noteworthy and regrettable that the only stakeholders in the regulated companies are perceived to be the consumers and the shareholders, with no mention of the workers. Gains from increased productivity appear to be the preserve of the shareholders and the customers rather than enabling higher wages to be paid.

A central feature of the Green Paper is that:

> RPI–*x* should be retained as the fundamental basis for price regulation, if the regulators consider this best serves consumers' interests. We also invite views on whether RPI–*x* could be supplemented with clear and in-built mechanisms to share unearned benefits promptly between consumers and shareholders when companies benefit from specific factors outside their control, or when they have deliberately misled the regulator by providing incomplete or inaccurate information when the price cap was set.

In those cases where the 'unearned benefits' arose from a sharp fall in the price of key inputs, this approach would have some attractions, though noting that sharp rises in input prices would presumably lead to price rises. However, the identification in practice of 'specific factors' outside the control of companies is problematic: for example how is an unexpected technological innovation which reduces costs to be regarded? Further, would faster than expected productivity growth arising from an increased work load on employees or from enhanced training and skills be regarded as an 'earned benefit' which can feed directly into profits? This approach would involve a considerable increase in the surveillance work of the regulatory agencies, and would also detract from the declared objective of 'securing a long-term, stable and effective framework'.

CONCLUDING REMARKS

There will be a continuing requirement for regulation of the utilities if they remain in private ownership, even in those areas where competition is being introduced. The task of regulation may become increasingly complex as companies diversify into activities outside of the utilities and as attention falls on issues such as quality of service and on universal supply obligations. There are some endemic problems which regulation faces. The first has been indicated above, namely the collection of relevant and accurate information on which price controls and quality of service obligations can be based.

The second is that regulation by its nature seeks to regulate and to constrain. In a sense there is regulation in order to prevent private companies from doing what they would otherwise have done (in this context particularly in the realm of prices). Regulation by its nature does not readily encourage new developments and innovations. In particular, it is difficult to ensure that investment takes place at an adequate rate and provides sufficient capacity to meet the peaks of demand. A profit seeking company will generally undertake investment when it perceives that the expected rate of return on that investment exceeds, by some margin and with due allowance for the riskiness of the investment, the rate of return which can be obtained on other forms of investment. The regulation of prices and profits is then constrained to ensure that the private utilities are securing rates of return which they deem sufficient to underpin future investment.

The third is that regulation involves significant costs: the operating costs of the regulatory agencies (include the MMC), as well as the compliance costs for the regulated utilities. For the reasons indicated above, these costs may well increase over time. Alternative modes of regulation (such as public ownership), of course, also involve costs, but we should be aware that the present system of regulation is not without its own costs.

5

PRACTICAL CONSTRAINTS ON PUBLIC OWNERSHIP

INTRODUCTION

This chapter considers a range of obstacles which appear to confront the restoration of the utilities to public ownership. Many of these obstacles would also confront an extension of public ownership. The precise form and difficulty of the obstacles varies between different forms of public ownership, but nevertheless arise in some way for each of the options considered in Chapter 7.

The first obstacle to consider is the perceived cost of the government re-purchasing the assets of the privatised utilities. It is assumed that the return of those assets to the public sector without compensation is not a practical possibility. Apart from the political difficulties of nationalisation without compensation (arising from, for example, the perception of the losses to pension funds and hence to pensioners), there would be many legal difficulties under European legislation, in particular Article 1 of the First Protocol of the European Convention of Human Rights.

Legal constraints, particularly those coming from European legislation, comprise the second obstacle. Articles 85 and 86 of the Treaty of Rome govern competition policy while Articles 92 to 94 govern state aid. Although these Articles would have some bearing on public ownership (e.g. monopoly positions arise in the distribution of electricity; there are loss-limits on public enterprise), they would not appear to create major obstacles to public ownership.

The third obstacle arises from the current and emerging structure of the utility industries. The significant dimensions of that structure are vertical disintegration, competition in gas and electricity supply, cross-ownership between sectors and diversification. These dimensions raise three major questions which need to be resolved.

First, what would the appropriate structure of the industries be under public ownership? This does not imply that the same basic structure would necessarily be appropriate for all the industries, and indeed the general view here would be that different structures (in terms of degree of vertical integration, and whether organised at a local, regional or national level) are likely to be appropriate for different industries. Vertical disintegration is considered in further detail in the next chapter.

Second, the vertically disintegrated nature of many public utility industries (notably gas and railways) raises the question of which parts of those industries should be returned to public ownership. For example, in the case of the railways, it would be technically feasible to restore Railtrack to public ownership (on the basis that the rail network is a natural monopoly) and leave some or all of the operating companies in private ownership.

Third, the increasingly diversified nature of the privatised utility companies (in terms of the products which they sell and the geographical spread, especially overseas, of their operations) would mean that not all the assets and operations of these companies should necessarily be returned to, and retained in, public ownership.

Clearly, the considerations for the return of British Gas to public ownership relate to its UK operations; whether or not British Gas under public ownership should continue to operate overseas is a separate matter. The scope of operation of a public enterprise would have to be decided on a case by case basis. The criterion should be: what does the British public gain from such overseas operations?

The fourth group of obstacles arises from the nature of the ownership of the privatised utility companies. In one dimension, this refers to the extent to which shares in these companies have remained in the hands of individuals, financial institutions or foreign owners. In another dimension, it refers to the extent to which the privatised utilities are wholly owned by other, notably foreign, companies. The political pressures which arise from these dimensions of ownership have to be considered. Ownership by financial institutions is often by pension funds, and public ownership would no doubt be represented as affecting people's pension rights (though this would not be the case where government bonds are issued in exchange for the shares of the nationalised company). The public ownership of utilities owned by foreign companies (which in most cases means American companies) will obviously be subject to counter pressure from the foreign government concerned.

FINANCIAL COSTS OF PUBLIC OWNERSHIP

Public ownership, and particularly the restoration of utilities to the public sector, is often dismissed on grounds of cost and the displacement of other desirable forms of expenditure, such as on the NHS or on education and training. However, this argument rests on a confusion between public expenditure which generates future revenue for the government (of which the purchase of utilities would be a major example) and other forms of public expenditure which do not directly generate future revenue. It is useful to start by drawing distinctions between three categories of public expenditure.

The first category, which forms the bulk of public expenditure, can be termed current expenditure on the provision of goods and services such as health care or education, and on transfer payments such as social security benefits. The former involves the use of resources to provide goods and services, whereas the latter is a transfer to the recipients: this is a relevant distinction in other contexts but does not need to detain us here.

The second category can be termed capital expenditure on non-revenue producing capital assets, which is the main form of public capital expenditure, and would include spending on, for example, new hospitals, roads or schools. This form of capital expenditure does not directly produce any additional revenue for the government, though there may be some indirect effects whereby, for example, road building helps to improve the supply-side of the economy which may lead to higher national income, and thereby taxation, in the future. Indeed, in many cases present capital expenditure may add to future current expenditure: for example more hospitals lead to provision of more health services in the future, and the employment of more medical staff etc. Public capital expenditure is intended to generate benefits for the public, but those benefits are not reflected in the revenue of the government.

The third category is capital expenditure on revenue-producing assets, which by definition produce additional revenue from the sale of the output produced from the capital equipment thereby acquired. The construction of roads on which tolls were charged would, for example, be included here. This category does not usually involve much public expenditure, but the acquisition of private sector companies would be included here. The key feature here is that what is produced by these assets is sold (e. g. tolls charged, gas sold) and the revenue from those sales helps to generate profits for the public sector.

While both forms of capital expenditure (and indeed current expenditure) have to be financed, their implications for future budget positions are quite different. Non-revenue producing capital expenditure may well create obligations for further expenditure in the future, whereas revenue-producing capital expenditure creates future income for the government. In cases where future income generated by a project is greater than interest charges on the loan to finance the project, the government is in effect profiting, and the government's revenue is raised by more than its costs. This should not be taken as an argument for government charging individuals fees for the services, which it provides: it is rather to indicate the different implications for the government's budget position.

Extension of public ownership has in the past generally involved compulsory exchange of shares in the company being taken into public ownership for interest-bearing bonds issued by the government. In many cases, the bonds are issued in the name of the publicly owned company, and interest payments on the bonds are clearly a charge against the profits of that company. In the case of the Attlee government nationalisation, much of the compensation in the case of electricity (often paid to local authorities as previous owners) was stock issued by the British Electricity Authority and in the case of gas by the Gas Council. In other cases, bonds are issued in the name of the government, and interest payments become a charge against general taxation.

The difference between the two cases is not a major one: bonds are generally considered as underwritten by the government, and in the unlikely event of the publicly owned company being unable to meet interest charges or make any required repayments, these would be paid by the government (or, equivalently, the resulting deficit of the publicly owned company would be financed by government).

This method of purchasing a company involves exchanging one set of paper providing income to the holders (share certificates) for another set of paper providing income (bonds). There is no substantial immediate cost to the government, though there will be some costs of organising the bonds issue and purchasing the private company. There will, though, be the commitment to make future interest payments on the bonds. Shareholders exchange one form of income-generation (shares) for another (bonds). The government is committed to future interest payments but has received in return the stream of income from the publicly owned company. Whether or not the government has gained clearly depends on how the future stream of interest payments compares with the future stream of profits. Making such a comparison is not straightforward, notably because any future stream of profits is inherently uncertain and because the level of investment within the publicly owned company is likely to be different from what it was under private ownership, and may be financed in different ways (whether from retained profits or further borrowing).

Interest payments will generally be fixed in nominal terms (that is as a fixed percentage of the price paid by government for the nationalised industry), whereas profits are likely to rise in line with inflation (though not necessarily at the same rate), as prices charged by the now nationalised industry rise. But two particularly crucial questions arise: was the price paid for the nationalised industry a reasonable one? and will the scale of profits be similar under nationalisation as under privatisation? The general run of evidence on the relative performance of privately owned and publicly owned companies, as discussed in Chapter 3, does not support any particular superiority of the efficiency of the private sector over the public sector. Reported profits will differ according to the toughness of the degree of price control that is exercised. It would be essential that any tightening of price control should be undertaken prior to the company being acquired for public ownership. The degree of price control will affect future profits prospects and hence the share price of the company. What must be avoided is the government paying a relatively high price for the company, followed by price restraint on the public enterprise and resulting low profits. This would entail relatively high interest charges (on the bonds to finance the high price paid) and relatively low profits to service those interest charges.

The reported profits of a public enterprise may also be lower when the enterprise is required to pay attention to a range of social purposes which may raise its costs without any compensation on its revenue. These social purposes may range widely, from concern over the environment to services to remote areas. Here, again, this is not to argue that public enterprises should not be run with regard to broader considerations than 'the bottom line', but the effects on the financial position of the public enterprise have to be considered.

Prices paid in previous nationalisations have typically been generous to shareholders. In the case of industries such as water and railways, which are subject to regulation of output price, the value of the companies involved is crucially dependent on the laxity of regulation. Thus it would make little financial sense for a government to nationalise a company and then impose a more severe degree of regulation on the company (or impose on the nationalised company social obligations which reduce its profits). It would make more sense to impose those more severe regulations and further obligations prior to taking the company concerned into public ownership so that the price which has to be paid for the company is correspondingly reduced.

The valuation of companies to be nationalised is not a straightforward matter. In the case of independent quoted companies, the stock market valuation is the starting point, and a benchmark against which the adequacy of compensation is likely to be judged by the Courts. Stock market valuation is subject to considerable fluctuation, and a high price could be paid for a company if acquisition by the government takes place at a time when that stock individually, or the stock market generally, is over valued.

The stock market price may be influenced by, for example, announcements on future dividend policies, or forecasts on profits growth. Further, suppose the current share price is £x, and nationalisation is in prospect; some in the stock market believe that the government will have to pay something above the current price (to ensure that compensation is deemed adequate) – let us call that premium dx. Then those in the stock market with that belief would be prepared to pay up to £$x + dx$, which would help to bid up the price towards £$x + dx$, which in turn pushes up the compensation figure towards £$x + dx + dx$ (as the government has to pay a premium above the market price). It only requires something of this effect to work for the share price to be bid up, thereby raising the compensation which the government has to pay. It is often reported that the impact of some event has been anticipated and is already incorporated into the share price of a company: this argument illustrates that idea, with the prospect of government acquisition of a company influencing the share price upwards.

In the case of utilities which are the wholly-owned subsidiary of other companies, the valuation is a more complex exercise. The ease with which government can get the valuation wrong is well illustrated by much of the privatisation programme. An example which has recently come to light is the losses on rolling stock as part of rail privatisation. The National Audit Commission reported the sale of three companies to the private sector for around £1.8 billion; these companies were later re-sold for a substantial profit; the value of their future cash flows under continuing public ownership would have been £2.9 billion (National Audit Office, Press Notice, 5 March 1998).

Taking a company into public ownership involves the transfer of ownership of the assets concerned from one group of people to another. Public ownership does not involve to any significant extent the use of resources. It is akin to a person buying a house from someone else compared with a person buying a new house. As such, it would have little or no effect on the level of aggregate demand in the economy, and should have little or no effect on the general budget position of the government. That is the level of taxation and other forms of public expenditure should be virtually unaffected by taking a company into public ownership.

The reasoning for this is as follows: wealth may have some effect on consumer expenditure – generally more wealth leads to more consumption expenditure – but the wealth position of the private sector is unchanged: shares have been swapped for bonds of an equivalent value. In this case, the public sector does not add to the demand for resources since all that is involved is a transfer of ownership. The analogy could be drawn that whereas the construction of a new house requires resources of people and materials and adds to the level of demand, the sale of an existing house does not.

The proceeds of privatisation were treated as negative public expenditure in government accounts, with a consequent reduction in the public sector borrowing requirement. It would have been more appropriate to treat the sale of assets as a means of financing part of the budget deficit; but it was a matter of 'selling the family silver' to finance a deficit, and as such it was a method which cannot be used indefinitely, as eventually all the silver will be disposed of. In the case of privatisation, a better analogy would have been the selling of parts of the family business, in that it was productive revenue producing assets which were being disposed of. Privatisation was in effect the exchange of productive assets for cash.

The issue of bonds by the government would add to the national debt, and hence raise the ratio of national debt to national income. But while the liabilities of the state (bonds) have increased, so have the assets (those of the now publicly owned company) and the net wealth position of the government has not changed.

It can be argued that the rise in the national debt to national income ratio has some detrimental effects. First, it would be marginally more difficult to satisfy the Maastricht criteria for convergence, of a debt to income ratio of 60 per cent. This suggests a deficiency in the Maastricht criteria in making no allowance for a government's assets and focusing on the gross rather than net liability position. However the rationale of the Maastricht criteria is that there should be a long term consistency between the deficit to income ratio and the debt to income ratio (figures of 3 per cent and 60 per cent are given which are consistent provided that the nominal growth rate is 5 per cent). A one-off increase in the gross liability (but not the net liability) position does not impact on those calculations. It should also be noted that many of the countries who are deemed to meet the criteria for inclusion in the single currency fail on the debt to income ratio test, and have debt to income ratios considerably above the 60 per cent level, whereas the current British ratio is significantly below 60 per cent.

The second difficulty relates to the workings of the financial markets. It can be argued that if a firm or industry were brought into full public ownership then the number of outstanding government bonds would be greater than otherwise, and the interest rate which the British government would have to pay on subsequent bond issues would be higher. In effect, the argument is that financial markets will absorb more British government bonds only if the price of the bonds is lower, and since the interest rate and the price of bonds are inversely related, this would mean a higher rate of interest. The public ownership of the water industry would involve the issue of bonds to the value of say around £25 to £30 billions (if based on current stock market prices) which compares with a national debt currently of around £400 billions (see note at end of chapter). While this argument about the effect on the interest rate which the British government would have to pay could be applicable, it is difficult to believe that a relatively small proportionate increase in British government bonds would have any marked effect on the price of those bonds. Further, as remarked earlier, the net liability position of the government does not change with the extension of public ownership, and in that respect the credit rating of the government should not change.

The enactment of the necessary legislation for public ownership does take Parliamentary time and other legislation would be displaced by that devoted to public ownership. This is a clear matter of political priorities. There would be some one-off re-organisation costs for the industry, which have to be balanced against the benefits of its being publicly owned. However, the financial costs of nationalisation, and the displacement of other forms of expenditure such as on the health service or on education should not be included amongst the serious considerations concerning the desirability or otherwise of re-nationalisation.

There are many objections which can be raised against the criteria of the Maastricht Treaty that budget deficit should not exceed 3 per cent of GDP, and government debt 60 per cent of GDP, but two related points are significant. First, when defining budget deficit as the difference between tax revenue and public expenditure, no distinction is made between current expenditure and capital expenditure. Thus borrowing to finance capital expenditure is treated in the same way as borrowing to finance current expenditure. For many purposes, this distinction between current expenditure and capital expenditure is not pertinent: whether it is current or capital expenditure, it still has to be paid for. In general, neither current nor capital expenditure leads directly to an increase in future government revenue which would contribute to paying the interest on any borrowing.

However, in the case of the restoration of public ownership the distinction is relevant for two reasons. First, the expenditure for the public ownership of a particular industry is 'one-off', and it is reasonable to spread the costs of 'one-off' expenditure over time as most of us do when purchasing a house with a mortgage. Borrowing to finance public ownership in effect spreads out the costs: the government borrows now but has to pay future interest charges and may eventually have to retire the debt (though there is the possibility of continually rolling over it). Second, as argued above, nationalisation involves a cost (acquiring the assets) but also generates a future stream of income (profits of the nationalised industry) with which to pay interest charges. In this respect, capital expenditure on income-producing assets is rather different from capital expenditure on other assets (such as schools or hospitals) which do not directly yield income to the government.

The second point relating to the Maastricht criteria is that a concern over the debt position of the government overlooks any corresponding assets of the government and the nature of those assets. It is ridiculous to set a limit on the national debt (such as 60 per cent of GDP) without paying regard to the scale of capital assets owned by the government (which often exceeds the debt) or to the question of whether those assets yield income to the government. At the end of 1996, the net wealth of central government was estimated by government statisticians to be -£178.6 billion (i.e. financial liabilities exceeded tangible and financial assets); local government was estimated to have net wealth of +£198.6 billion; and with the public corporations the overall net wealth of the public sector amounted to +£64.9 billion.

The government has committed itself to two fiscal rules, namely: 'the golden rule: over the economic cycle the Government will borrow only to invest and not to fund current expenditure' (Treasury, 1997, p1) – though capital consumption (depreciation) is regarded as current spending so that it is net capital formation which can be financed by borrowing. Secondly, 'public debt as a proportion of national income will be held over the economic cycle at a stable and prudent level' (p1).

Further, 'the fiscal rules focus on the whole of the public sector, because the debts of any part of the public sector could ultimately fall on the taxpayer. Looking at the whole public sector also removes incentives to reclassify activities simply to evade prudent constraints on borrowing' (p16). This would clearly suggest that borrowing by public enterprises would be covered by these fiscal rules. Public enterprises are likely to make a net positive contribution to the budget position. Throughout, nationalised companies made a substantial operating profit, and made considerable payments of interest and dividends. These companies were also undertaking a large investment programme. The net result was that for much of the 1970s and early 1980s the nationalised industries added to the borrowing requirement of the government, but from the mid 1980s onwards were in substantial financial surplus.

The 'golden rule' itself does not say anything about the scale of capital expenditure, only that it may be financed through borrowing (over the cycle). On those grounds, since the acquisition of assets through nationalisation should count as a capital expenditure by the government, the 'golden rule' would not prevent the extension of public ownership. Indeed, the 'golden rule' would explicitly allow borrowing (the issue of bonds) to finance the capital expenditure of acquiring assets. Public ownership would, though, constitute an increase in outstanding public debt (though as indicated above offset by an increase in the assets of the public sector). The increase in public debt would not be a continuous one but more like a one-off increase as the nationalisation takes place (though that may be spread over a number of years). What is meant by a 'prudent level' of debt is not specified (though the terms of the Stability and Growth Pact governing the European single currency may be in mind, that is debt equivalent to 60 per cent of GDP or less). But if 'prudent' relates to the government's ability to finance interest payments on the debt, then, as we have argued above, that is unaffected by nationalisation as interest payments to be made by the government are counter balanced by the profits on the public enterprises.

We conclude that because public ownership of utilities would generate revenue which can readily cover the interest payments associated with taking those utilities back into public ownership, there is no displacement of other forms of public expenditure.

EUROPEAN LEGISLATION

There are many areas of European legislation which could potentially affect public ownership of the utilities and other companies. Some of these we could only speculate about as there may be obscure pieces of law which potentially could be used to delay or change proposals for public ownership. However since the utilities are publicly owned in many European Union member countries, it is unlikely that European legislation would pose a complete constraint on public ownership. Indeed, Article 222 of the Treaty of Rome states that 'this treaty shall in no way prejudice the rules in Member Sates governing the system of property ownership'. The aspects of public ownership on which European legislation could impact relate to competition and monopoly, state aid and subsidies, employment practices and compensation to previous owners.

Articles 85 and 86 of the Treaty of Rome constitute the basis of a monopoly and mergers policy in the European Union: Article 85 deals with cartels and restrictive trade practices and Article 86 with monopoly. These articles refer to inter-state trade, which would appear to exclude any cartels or monopolies affecting only within-country trade, but the articles also cover agreements and actions which serve to limit imports from one EC country to another.

Article 86 deals with the abuse of market dominance rather than with monopoly per se, and with those abuses which affect trade between member states. In the Article, particular abuses mentioned are:

> (a) directly or indirectly imposing unfair purchase or selling prices or other unfair trading conditions;
> (b) limiting production, markets or technical development to the prejudice of consumers;
> (c) applying dissimilar conditions to equivalent transactions with other trading parties, thereby placing them at a competitive disadvantage;

(d) making the conclusion of contracts subject to acceptance by the other parties of supplementary obligations which, by their nature or according to commercial usage, have no connection with the subject of such contracts (part of Article 86 of the Treaty of Rome).

The Treaty of Rome does not define dominance but the Court has looked at both market share and actions before arriving at a view as to whether there is dominance in a particular case. A market share as low as 40 per cent has been used as partial evidence of dominance. There is the problem of finding an appropriate definition of the market, and this problem is exacerbated in the EC context since the question arises as to whether the appropriate market area is the whole of the EC or is one particular country or region.

Article 90 covers the 'revenue producing monopoly' and states that such a monopoly 'shall be subject to the rules contained in this Treaty, in particular to the rules on competition, in so far as the application of such rules does not obstruct the performance in law or in fact, of the particular tasks assigned to them'. This article clearly permits a wide range of latitude by the reference to the 'particular tasks assigned to them', and it covers revenue producing monopolies, whether privately or publicly owned.

Articles 92 to 94 of the Treaty of Rome restrict state aid to firms, whether in the private or public sector. The range of state aid which is covered has been defined to be constituted not only by grants, 'but also by loans on more favourable terms than are available on the market, guarantees, tax concessions, relief of social security contributions, and by the state putting up new capital for enterprises in circumstances in or on terms which a private investor would not do so' (Commission of the European Communities, *Fourteenth Report on Competition Policy*, Brussels: Office for Official Publications of the European Communities, 1985).

Part of Article 92 makes state aid which distorts (or threatens to distort) competition by favouring some firms or industries in so far as trade between member countries is affected incompatible with the common market. It also provides a list of aid which is compatible with the common market and others which may be so considered. Article 93 leads to state aid being kept under constant review, with member countries having to report plans on state aid. The impact of Articles 92 to 94 on the subsequent operation of public ownership would arise if the provision of finance by government to public enterprise was deemed to be 'on more favourable terms than are available on the market'. A strict interpretation of this could lead to limits on the provision of finance by government to workers' co-operatives which find difficulty in obtaining finance from the private sector.

We would conclude from this brief review that the monopoly and competition policy of the European Union would have no direct impact on public ownership. The limitations on state aid would similarly have little impact (in part as it would not be envisaged that utilities would require state aid).

LEGAL CONSTRAINTS

The possible legal constraints on public ownership arise from the complexity of legislation needed to bring about the desired outcomes, and limitations which arise from European law. UNISON has already sought legal opinion from Lord Wedderburn of Charlton QC on the legal issues involved in the return of utilities to the public sector. His opinion is reproduced as Appendix 3 of UNISON report, *The Privatised Utilities* (NEC Report Number Two, 1996). Some of these have been touched on above as some of the legal issues that arise from UK membership of the European Union (and the associated European Court of Justice), and we do not repeat the discussion on the European legal issues.

The following issues stand out from that legal opinion. First, and most importantly, Lord Wedderburn concludes: 'there is no constitutional or other legal reason, in these Acts [those concerned with the privatisation of electricity, gas and water industries] or elsewhere, which would totally prohibit a future government from bringing back the utilities into public ownership, for example by vesting their assets in public corporations or similar bodies. The primary questions on that issue are of course political, not legal'. He notes that the Secretary of State has 'extensive powers to make delegated legislation or other binding orders or decision under these Acts ... But in my view such powers in the various Acts now on the statute book manifestly do not extend to the compass, or anything like the compass, which would be required to bring all the utilities back into public ownership' (p57). He concludes: 'the only method of bringing that result about (utilities back into public ownership) would be for Parliament to enact primary legislation'. Further, 'it would not be practicable for a re-nationalisation statue to be composed merely of such clauses [which give the Minister power to do virtually what he likes]' (pp57-8).

Second, Lord Wedderburn states that it has become increasingly difficult for legislation on public ownership to avoid the form of a 'hybrid' bill ('a Bill affecting specific private rights as well as public policy, which needs to undergo special procedures, causing great delay', p58).

Third, there is the issue of the level of compensation for assets taken into public ownership. It may be recalled that the legislation on the nationalisation of the aircraft and shipbuilding industries in the 1970s was subject to prolonged litigation on these lines. Lord Wedderburn notes that the foreign ownership of some of the utility companies complicates these questions. Compensation would have to be pitched at a level which avoids contravention of Article 1 of the First Protocol of the European Convention of Human Rights. This would seem to remove any possibility of nationalisation without compensation or subject only to some criteria of need.

Fourth, 'some Member States of the European Union which have attempted to find a short cut to public control have been restrained by the European Court of Justice under the Treaties from pursuing that course' (p58), and the example cited arises from Greece in 1983. The Greek government set up the Business Reconstruction Organisation ('OAE'), which was a public limited company controlled by the state which could take over private sector companies in order to rejuvenate them.

Future limitations could well arise from the Multilateral Agreement on Investment (MAI) which is currently being negotiated at the Organisation for Economic Co-operation and Development (OECD). The discussion here is based on the draft text of 14 February 1998, taken from the web site mai.flora.org. The MAI is designed to limit the powers of governments to restrict and regulate foreign investment, and as such the agreement, if implemented, could affect the possibilities for future public ownership of foreign-owned utilities, as well as their regulation. The MAI would apply first to OECD countries and then to other countries as they become signatories. The provision of this agreement which is particularly relevant here is that which would ban uncompensated expropriation of assets. The draft text states that

> a contracting party shall not expropriate or nationalise directly or indirectly an investment in its territory of an investor of another Contracting Party or take any measure or measures having equivalent

effect (hereinafter referred to as 'expropriation') except:

a) for a purpose which is in the public interest,
b) on a non-discriminatory basis,
c) in accordance with due process of law, and
d) accompanied by payment of prompt, adequate and effective compensation. Compensation shall be paid without delay.

Compensation shall be equivalent to the fair market value of the expropriated investment immediately before the expropriation occurred. The fair market value shall not reflect any change in value occurring because the expropriation had become publicly known earlier. Compensation shall be fully realisable and freely transferable

(from Section IV, 2 of the draft agreement)

This could have implications not only for public ownership, but also for the regulation of privatised utilities. Expropriation can be taken here to include not just seizure of property and assets but also government action which is deemed equivalent to expropriation. Property is broadly defined to include, *inter alia*, intellectual property rights, licences and concessions. Thus it could be argued that certain forms of regulation are equivalent to expropriation, requiring governments to compensate investors for lost revenue. Thus tightening regulation which led to a reduction in the rate of profit (or indeed regulations relating to environmental protection which led to a loss of revenue) could be construed as falling under this provision. Some environmental campaigners have also seen these provisions as potentially limiting environmental regulation.

We may conclude from this that there are no insuperable legal limitations on public ownership, though the precise form of that ownership and the levels of compensation are constrained by legal considerations. It does suggest that Parliamentary time for the restoration of public ownership may be substantial and that drafting the legislation may face many pitfalls.

STRUCTURE OF PRIVATISED UTILITIES

Many of the nationalised industries were vertically integrated statutory monopolies. Since privatisation there have been many changes (besides that of the switch from public to private ownership) which may have some bearing on the possibility of bringing companies back into public ownership, and which raise questions about the form which public ownership should take. 'It is clear ... that all three utilities today bear little resemblance to the electricity and gas industries nationalised in the late 1940s as monolithic bodies and to the water industry, reorganised and restructured in the 1970s and 1980s' (UNISON, 1996, p8). The structural changes include vertical disintegration, diversification and the introduction of competition, and we now discuss these in turn.

The process of privatisation was often accompanied by the vertical disintegration of the industries concerned. This has been particularly noticeable in the case of the railways with the separation between the rail operating companies, the rolling stock leasing companies and Railtrack. It is also apparent in the case of gas and electricity, with the separation between electricity generation and its transmission, and the separation of the supply of gas, the distribution of gas and supply of repair services. The rationale for this disintegration is discussed in the next chapter. Here, it is sufficient to note that this vertical disintegration has often been associated with attempts to introduce competition in some parts of the overall supply chain. Vertical disintegration also involves costs of co-ordination between different parts of the supply chain, a co-ordination which previously had been undertaken within the larger vertically integrated organisation.

Many privatised utilities have moved towards diversification, including overseas operations and away from the 'core' business. Many nationalised industries were restricted in their activities, but no such restrictions exist for privatised companies. There is no particular reason to think that the privatised companies will restrict themselves to their initial core business. Indeed in so far as their core business generates substantial profits, but where that business does not face a rapid growth of demand or technological change, those companies will be looking for expansion opportunities outside of the core business.

Diversification makes regulation of the core business more difficult. The allocation of shared costs between the regulated part of the business and the non-regulated part becomes problematic, and there are clear possibilities for moving accounting profits out of the regulated part into the non-regulated part. There is the clear danger that, with the passage of time, the utility-based part of the operation will become peripheral to the company's interests as it diversifies into other unregulated and perhaps more profitable areas. While community interest lies with the low-cost provision of utilities, the interests of the businesses may lie elsewhere. This danger was highlighted by UNISON as follows:

> Although the water companies will continue to provide water and sewerage services as their core responsibilities, all the signs are that they are looking more and more towards the unregulated non-core parts of the business as sources of profit. Since privatisation the number of subsidiary companies set up to promote non-core commercial activities has increased substantially. Many of these are concerned with property development, financial services and insurance. Most are registered and operate within the UK, but there is an increasing number abroad in countries as diverse as Australia, Malaysia, Mexico and Poland. The water companies will be looking to increase these activities, both as sources of profits and as a means of evading regulation (UNISON 1996, p38).

Some of the dangers are illustrated by the recent experience in Auckland with a 'blackout (which) is unprecedented in the developed world'. In the Auckland area, 'Mercury Energy had been privatised with little public support and even less government control ... And there is the firm belief the company has spent its time and energy on corporate matters rather than on smaller things – such as maintenance of cables ... the business community, chief advocates of privatisation, are now its chief victims' (*Observer* 8 March 1998).

The particular difficulty which diversification raises for public ownership is the specification of the assets which are to be acquired. It may not be simply a matter of acquiring company X since that company may be producing a range of goods and services as well as, say, distributing electricity in a particular region. It is a matter of seeking to acquire the assets used in the distribution of electricity in that region. This should not be an insurmountable problem since, for example, the pre-nationalised rail companies operated a range of other services such as hotels, cross-channel ferries and road haulage, and after nationalisation some of those services remained in the public sector.

A further and recent structural change has been the introduction of competition in the production of electricity and in the supply and shipping of gas, while their distribution to the consumer remain as monopolies. The emerging competition in the production of electricity and the supply of gas poses a number of considerations for public ownership. The first consideration arises from acknowledging that, while the transmission of electricity and gas is a natural monopoly (in the sense that the costs of multiple transmission networks would be much higher than the costs of a single network without any corresponding benefits), the actual production of electricity and supply of gas is not. In both cases, production is not subject to extensive economies of scale, and hence both can be produced on a relatively small scale (that is small relative to the market for electricity or gas). From that perspective, it would be possible to have numerous producers and suppliers. The vertical disintegration of an industry involves significant transaction costs, but also has the potential to introduce competition in some of the stages of production. But many would question the extent of competition under these circumstances, and would predict that the number of alternative producers will be relatively small.

The restoration of those industries, in whole or in part, to public ownership would raise a number of questions relating to competition. The first is: should gas supply and electricity generation only be undertaken by the nationalised industry (perhaps subject to some minor exceptions such as electricity generation for own use)? The second is: if existing production facilities were all taken into public ownership, could new privately owned production facilities be established in the future? This, in effect, raises the question of access to the distribution network. The third is: should public ownership involve competition between public enterprises?

These questions raise the issue of the appropriate structure of the electricity and gas industries under public ownership. We will return to this in later chapters, but clearly there are (at least) three possible models. The first is the vertically integrated industry, similar to that which existed under nationalisation. The second is the public ownership of only part of the industry such as the transmission network, with other parts such as gas or electricity production remaining privatised and undertaken competitively. The third is public ownership of the whole system but not within a unified framework. This could mean, for example, that the national grid, distribution and production in the case of electricity were all under public ownership but with the national grid as a national monopoly, distribution as a number of regional monopolies and competitive public ownership for production.

Another consideration is the added complexity which would be created for public ownership. It may be recalled that when the Attlee government nationalised electricity and gas, it took into (national) public ownership a mixture of locally-owned and private companies in the cases of gas and electricity (with the already publicly owned national grid, completed in 1935). The renationalisation of a monopoly would clearly be much more straightforward and would not run into complications associated with anti-monopoly legislation.

OWNERSHIP OF THE UTILITIES

When the utilities were privatised, the government sought to ensure that a significant proportion of the shares in the privatised companies were allocated to individual shareholders, and in a number of cases further shares were allocated to individuals (and away from the financial institutions) because of the high demand for shares from the public. This was perhaps most effectively summarised in the publicity over the privatisation of gas which focused as 'telling Sid'. One of the effects of the privatisation programme does appear to have been the increase in the number of shareholders (which has been added to by the de-mutualisation of Building Societies). Estimates vary from something of the order of 5-7 per cent of the adult population to around 20 per cent. However, the impact here of privatisation appears to be of shareholders with a small holding of shares in one or two companies.

The proportion of shares owned directly by individuals has tended to decline throughout the post-war period; ownership by financial institutions (mainly banks, unit trusts, pension funds and insurance companies) continued to grow during the 1980s with the proportion of shares held by individuals declining from 30.4 per cent at the end of 1981 to 20.3 per cent in 1993 (figures taken from CSO, *Share Register Survey Report*, London: HMSO 1991, and 'The 1993 share register survey', *Economic Trends*, October 1993). In 1993 the beneficial owners of the privatised companies were central government 9.2 per cent (compared with 1.4 per cent in all companies), pension funds 27.6 per cent (33.0 per cent in all companies), insurance companies 12.4 per cent (15.7 per cent), unit trusts 4.5 per cent (5.9 per cent), individuals 24.5 per cent (20.3 per cent), overseas 8.3 per cent (12.1 percent), and others 12.1 per cent (9.6 per cent). The government's holdings will have decreased since those figures were compiled, and the overseas ownership increased, as discussed below. But those figures suggest that share holding by individuals in privatised companies is similar in scale to share holding in other companies, though individuals with shares in privatised companies may have few other share holdings.

Appendix 4 of UNISON (1996) gives a summary result of a shareholder search (28 November 1995 on six utility companies). For example Yorkshire Water reveals the following figures: (Table 5.1)

Group	Per cent
Insurance Companies	23.93
Pension Funds	15.64
Finance Companies	10.12
Banks	8.43
Local Authorities	2.64

In addition, the Church of England held 0.68 per cent, and H.M. Government 0.74 per cent. The identified holdings added up to 63.2 per cent of the issue. The figures given for other companies are not dissimilar.

The significance of these figures arises from the indirect interest which many people have in the value of these shares through their insurance policies and pension arrangements.

On privatisation, preference was given to UK-based shareholders and institutions in the allocation of shares, and there were some limits on the foreign take-over of privatised companies through the retention by the government of a 'golden share'. However, the 'golden shares' have lapsed and there are no limits on the subsequent sale of shares to foreign nationals or institutions. Subsequently, there has been a wave of acquisitions of utilities, some by other UK-based utilities, some by foreign-based utilities and others by non-utility companies. A (partial) list of the acquisitions is given in Table 2. Although it is not self-evident from that list, almost all of the acquiring companies are American based utilities and energy companies.

The nationality of the owners of companies to be taken into public ownership may be relevant for (at least) three reasons. First, in so far as control comes with ownership, foreign ownership implies foreign control. This may be more relevant in a case where a UK-based utility is fully owned by a foreign company which is thereby able to exercise control over the UK-based utility, rather than in a case where some of the shareholders are based outside the UK. Although it may seem far fetched, transnational companies do, on occasions, withdraw and close down production and distribution facilities in a country as well as opening them. Concern has been expressed by the Trade and Industry Committee over the consequences of failures of gas suppliers and shippers, though this could be as a result of the failure of a domestic or foreign owned enterprise (Trade and Industry Committee, 1998, pxxiii).

Table 5.2 Partial list of acquisitions amongst privatised utilities

Acquiring Company	Acquired Company
Southern Company of America	SWEB
Hanson Trust, then sold to Energy Group which has now been acquired by Texas	Eastern Group
Scottish Power	Manweb
North West Water	NORWEB
Central and South West Corporation of America	SEEB
Avon Energy	Midlands Electricity
CE Electric	Northern Electricity
Dominion Resources	East Midlands
Entergy	London Electricity
PS Colorado & AEP	Yorkshire Electricity
Scottish Power	Southern Water
Lyonnaise des Eaux	Northumbrian Water
Welsh Water	SWALEC

It is also a matter of concern that the utility is used as a 'cash cow' to generate profits which are invested elsewhere in the foreign corporation. In other words, there is relatively little investment in the UK-based utility. There is nothing within the current regulatory regime which ensures that a foreign owned (or indeed UK owned) utility continues in operation or that there is an adequate level of investment.

Second, as has already been indicated, the multilateral agreement on investment (MAI) imposes constraints on the level of compensation which would have to be paid, as well as possibly constraining the ability of the UK government to regulate the privatised utilities.

Third, the political forces against public ownership might be different, and in particular the government of the country in which the owners are located is likely to be involved. Since most of the take-overs of the RECs has been by American based companies, this means in effect the involvement of the American government.

Conclusions

Nothing which has been discussed in this chapter would prevent utilities and other industries being taken into public ownership. There are clearly limitations arising from the need for possibly complex Parliamentary legislation, but that is because of constraints of Parliamentary time and the ordering of government priorities. The cost of public ownership is largely a non-issue, as was amply demonstrated by the financing of the extensive nationalisation programme of the Attlee government. There are legal pitfalls which have to be avoided, and the constraints of European legislation would appear to rule out nationalisation without compensation broadly in line with the prevailing stock market valuations.

Note on valuation of water companies

The cost of acquiring the assets employed in, say, the water industry can only be approximated. Water companies operate outside of their core activities, and some have been acquired by other companies. However an order of magnitude is given by the stock market valuation of those water companies which are still separately listed on the Stock Exchange. At the end of May 1998, the stock market valuation of those eight companies was close to £20 billion, and with allowance for the two companies which have been acquired and for the smaller water only companies, the cost of public ownership of all the water and sewerage companies would be of the order of £25 to £30 billion under present conditions. The stock market valuation of the companies could be changed through speculation over public ownership and perhaps more significantly through the imposition of a tighter regulatory framework

6

EFFICIENCY, OWNERSHIP, AGENCY AND VERTICAL (DIS)INTEGRATION

INTRODUCTION

The overall purpose of this chapter is to briefly discuss some of the efficiency considerations related to private and public ownership, and some of the factors which should influence the structural form of public ownership. The underlying purpose of this discussion is to consider the design of forms of public ownership which would operate in an efficient and effective manner. Public ownership is of course concerned with more than mere efficiency, as the discussion in Chapter 2 should illustrate, but an inefficient and ineffective public sector serves no-one's interests.

We will make frequent reference to 'efficiency' in the discussion below. By efficiency we mean achieving the maximum output for given inputs (or equivalently minimising inputs to achieve a given output). We do not use the term 'improving efficiency' as a euphemism for reducing wages or increasing work intensity. Although increased efficiency will usually be reflected in increased profitability, it is not the case that increased profits necessarily mean increased efficiency (since, for example, wages may have been reduced or prices raised) nor that efficiency is only reflected in profitability. Public ownership will have wider objectives than private ownership: ultimately the former is concerned with the promotion of the general social interest and the latter with profits. The output of an industry is usually seen in terms of the amount of gas, electricity – or any other product – that is produced. But output of an industry should be much more broadly interpreted to include, for example, the conditions under which people work, or the universality of the service.

Private ownership is often perceived as being more efficient than public ownership, though as we have reported above the evidence does not support any such perceptions. Whilst a range of arguments has been deployed to back up that notion, there are three major ones. The first is that private ownership provides the incentive of profits to reduce costs and to promote efficient production. The second is that if a private company becomes lax, it will be punished by being taken over. The third is that it is competition which promotes efficiency, and that competition is usually associated with private rather than public ownership, and also that competition is only effective when firms are struggling over profits. We briefly examine these propositions in the next three sections, and suggest that they offer far from compelling reasons for private, rather than public, ownership.

In the next three sections we also consider issues related to the efficient operation of publicly owned companies. There are variations in efficiency and responsiveness amongst publicly owned enterprises (as there are amongst privately owned ones), which may suggest that some approaches to public ownership are better than others. This leads us to consideration of the setting of objectives for public enterprises, and to the vexed question of pay structure (and in particular performance related pay). The vertical disintegration of utilities following privatisation leads us to consider the desirability of that disintegration and whether or not public ownership should involve a vertically integrated industry.

In the last two sections, we turn to issues of democracy and accountability under public ownership.

Property rights and efficiency

There are many factors which influence an industry's level of efficiency, ranging from the skills and commitment of the workforce through to the competence of managers. There were also many forces which lay behind the privatisation programme of the Thatcher and Major governments, including a belief that privatisation would weaken trade unions. But a particularly significant reason behind the privatisation programme, even if it was not always fully spelled out, was the notion that private ownership was more efficient and involved lower costs than public ownership. This was then represented as private ownership improving efficiency, even though there were substantial effects resulting from the reduction of wages and the intensification of work. The evidence surveyed in Chapter 3 does not support the view that private ownership is generally more efficient than public ownership; the experience of privatisation has not been one of a general improvement in efficiency. In some cases it appears to have improved efficiency but not in others.

The argument that production under private ownership will be more efficient and will involve lower costs than under public ownership really amounts to the following notion. If an individual has rights to the surplus which is generated by some activity, then that person will run the activity with a view to gaining as large a surplus as possible, because that will give the individual as high an income as possible. Since the surplus of an activity is the difference between revenue and costs of that activity, then seeking to maximise the surplus implies seeking to increase revenues and/or reduce costs. In the literature, this has often been referred to as the importance of the 'residual claimant' to the surplus who acts as a 'monitor' over costs (Alchian and Demsetz, 1971). The 'residual claimant' then has incentives to reduce costs as much as possible, and thus, it is believed, the activity will be organised in an efficient manner.

Whatever the plausibility of this argument when applied to a small business owned and managed by one person, it is of dubious relevance to the case of the large business enterprise with numerous shareholders (who may be numbered in millions) and with a separation between ownership and control (management). Although it is an argument which has slipped out of fashion, many (of which Crosland, 1956, was a notable example) have argued that there are considerable similarities between large private companies and large public ones, with both facing problems of organising and operating a large organisation in an effective manner. From this, we would suggest that the form of ownership is not the key factor for efficiency; what is important is the way in which the company is organised and managed. This is not simply a matter of management style and organisational structure, but also of the involvement and participation of workers in decision making and implementation processes.

Ownership does become relevant when considering the objectives of an organisation. The private company may be run for a wide range of motives, but the pursuit of profits is usually a dominant one. The public company, in contrast, can pursue a much broader range of objectives, as we discuss below.

THE ROLE OF TAKE-OVERS

Public ownership removes the threat of being taken over (unless privatisation is retained as a threat!) which privately owned companies face. It is frequently argued that the threat of take-overs keeps firms (and particularly managers) on their toes, and that take-overs happen when a firm becomes 'slack' and another firm can take over the slack firm and improve its performance. The evidence on take-overs has tended to conclude that whilst there appear to be some gains for the shareholders of the company which is acquired, there is no general tendency for efficiency or profitability to be raised through take-over. Indeed, on balance, efficiency and profitability are harmed through take-over. A comparison of the larger firm after acquisition with a combination of the two firms involved prior to acquisition (with appropriate adjustments for changes in the general economic environment) reveals on average a decline in efficiency and profitability (e.g. Sawyer, 1985, Chapter 13, Fairburn and Kay, 1989). This has been a general finding, though it does refer to the average, and there are a significant minority of take-overs which appear to raise profitability and efficiency.

Take-overs are, at best, a costly and rather inefficient mechanism for disciplining the inefficient enterprise. They have the rather perverse effect that the main gainers from a take-over are the shareholders of the firm which is acquired. The absence of the threat of take-over under public ownership should not be a matter of any great regret.

COMPETITION AND EFFICIENCY

Many criticised the privatisation programme of the 1980s for its failure to inject competition into the industries concerned. Fine (1990) summarises this view when he writes that: 'the conclusion is drawn that the emphasis on state or private *ownership* of industry, as suggested by a debate over privatisation, is misplaced ... Ownership as such is seen as a secondary issue. Of much greater importance are the conditions governing competition and regulation' (p129). Public corporations which were statutory monopolies became privately owned monopolies. There were some minor exceptions to this; notably Mercury was established as a relatively small player in the telecommunications market. Privatising a company with its monopoly position intact presented the government with the advantage that the continuing monopoly position allowed high profits to be gained and high dividends to be paid in the future which led to a high share price for the company on flotation. This is even though companies were privatised at a substantial discount below their value, estimated to be generally of the order of 25 per cent (Vickers and Yarrow, 1989, pp173-180). The introduction of competition (or indeed a tough regulation regime) alongside privatisation would have placed doubts on future profits and dividends, and hence on the market price of the shares in the privatised company. The protection of the monopoly position also helped to retain the support of managers for privatisation because their position was not threatened and indeed the post-privatisation record on salaries shows that many managers gained substantially from privatisation.

Competition is seen by some as the spur to efficiency and as an incentive to provide goods which meet consumers' wishes, whereas others would see competition as forcing down costs which pushes down wages and working conditions. While acknowledging that these views are not entirely in conflict and may both contain some truth, the question is how relevant these considerations are for public ownership and the utilities. On the one hand, competition in the utility industries is likely to be rather limited. This is not only a reflection of the natural monopoly aspects of utilities which preclude competition, but also of the view that even in those aspects where competition is possible it is likely that there will only be a relatively small number of competitors. The experience in industries such as the bus and coach industry, where competition followed de-regulation, has been that, after the first flurry of competition, the industry evolved into one with a few dominant firms. 'Ten years on [after privatisation and deregulation of buses] three private sector companies control over 50 per cent of the market and the few remaining independents are continuing to be snapped up' (Siraut, 1997, p97).

On the other hand, in those areas of production and distribution where it is technically feasible for there to be a number of independent enterprises, it would be possible to have competition between publicly owned companies, or indeed between companies with different ownership characteristics. Competition does not have to involve private ownership (as the competition between universities illustrates).

OBJECTIVES AND PRICES

In this section, we draw on the experience of nationalisation to reflect on the setting of objectives for a public enterprise. A privatised company has one ultimate objective: that of profit. To pursue that objective may involve other goals – to ensure the company's survival, to act as a 'good employer' (or as a 'bad employer'), to pay attention to environmental considerations (or not), etc – but there is the single basic objective. Any service to the customer is a by-product of this pursuit of profits. In contrast, the publicly owned company can be given a range of objectives, which may include such things as breaking even or meeting a profits target, good employment practices, or high quality service.

It has often been said that publicly owned companies such as the nationalised industries have suffered from vague and/or conflicting objectives. Instructions to pursue the 'public interest' give little guidance to managers as to what they are striving to achieve, and provide little basis on which the performance of the managers can be assessed. The fuzziness of objectives was conducive to neither efficiency nor to accountability.

Some general features of the Attlee government's nationalisation programme have been summarised by a leading expert in the following terms:

> The Nationalisation Acts of 1945-8 had two central features. First was that the new corporations were to serve the public interest and hence a public purpose was written into the acts and embraced the provision of common services and the development of investment programmes. Thus the B.T.C. [British Transport Commission] was required to provide 'an efficient, adequate, economic and properly integrated system of public inland transport and port facilities' ... The N.C.B. [National Coal Board] was charged with securing 'the efficient development of the coal industry ... [and] ... making supplies of coal available ... as may seem to [the new Board] ... best calculated to serve the public interest, including the avoidance of any undue or unreasonable preference or advantage ... [and with] ... advancing the skill of persons employed.
>
> Consonant with these aims was the constitution of the boards, whose members were to be as disinterested as the corporations' objectives ...
>
> Secondly, the new undertakings were expected to be commercially oriented, innovative, and enterprising ... 'Cheap and efficiently supplied services' are words which recur in all the statutes and have to be taken with another injunction, variously worded, along the lines of 'revenues shall not be less than sufficient for meeting all outgoings properly chargeable, on an average of good and bad years. Vague though this wording might be for accountants, it was roundly considered to have the straightforward interpretation of breaking even, taking one year with another, as was much more easily monitored than the even vaguer public purposes' (Millward, 1997, pp229-230).

The nationalised industries were initially charged with breaking even on average. A White Paper in 1961 (*Financial and Economic Obligations of the Nationalised Industries*, Cmnd. 1337) introduced financial targets for public corporations, with target rates of return specified for each industry, but varying between industries depending on factors such as demand conditions and the degree to which the corporation was required to provide unprofitable services. A White Paper in 1967 (*Nationalised Industries: A Review of Economic and Financial Objectives*, Cmnd. 3437) made three significant innovations, while still requiring nationalised industries to meet a financial target. These were:

(i) the setting of prices to reflect long-run incremental (marginal) costs;
(ii) subjecting investment to a test discount rate of 8 per cent initially, later raised to 10 per cent (i.e. requiring a rate of return on investment of at least 8 (10) per cent);
(iii) identifying and seeking government funding for any non-commercial activities (e.g. rural train services).

The prices and incomes policies of the 1960s and 1970s brought limits on the prices of the nationalised industries as part of the anti-inflationary policies. In a number of cases, the imposed constraints on prices generated considerable losses for the industries, which helped to spread the idea of nationalised industries as loss makers and also obscured the measurement of performance of those industries.

The linking of prices with (incremental) costs was difficult to implement, and its role was downgraded with the White Paper of 1978 (*The Nationalised Industries*, Cmnd 7131). In this White Paper a framework of control was outlined in which the strategic objectives of the nationalised industries were agreed by the relevant government department, and within which financial control and planning were set. Investment was usually required to earn a 5 per cent rate of return in real terms (i.e. after allowing for inflation). In addition to financial targets, external financing limits (EFLs) were imposed, which in effect cover the cash flow (revenue minus current and capital expenditures) of public corporations. EFLs were included as part of the public sector borrowing requirement, though they could be negative (which would mean that the public corporation concerned was required to make a net contribution to the Exchequer) or positive. But these limits largely served to constrain capital expenditure, and concerns over the PSBR could feed back to limit investment. Financial targets, which often included a required rate of return, served to determine the level of prices relative to costs.

The requirement in much of the legislation on nationalisation that the public corporation should operate in the 'public interest' serves to remind us that the objectives of public ownership are broader than the 'bottom line' of profit and loss. However, the use of rather nebulous phrases such as 'public interest' does present problems. It can leave the interpretation of the 'public interest' in the hands of the managers of the public corporation, rather than with Parliament or some other representative forum. The lack of precision also makes it difficult to judge whether or not the public corporation has met its objectives and whether or not the 'public interest' has indeed been served. There is much to be said in favour of 'public interest' being more closely specified by Parliament so that Parliament itself can monitor the public corporation to ascertain whether its objectives have been met. Further, exactly what constitutes 'public interest' should vary between industries. For example, for the railways, the 'public interest' may include provision of services which are unprofitable but which meet a social need, as well as a high level of safety, whereas for the water industry it may include a universal service obligation, and an equitable pricing structure. In some cases, it would be appropriate for Parliament to enter into a specific contract with the public corporation. The clearest example of this was payment to British Rail for the provision of rail services in particular areas. In other cases this may not be appropriate. For example, it could be argued that rail passengers should bear the costs of higher safety requirements, and an equitable pricing structure could mean that some pay more and others less. Perceptions of what is the 'public interest' will no doubt change over time, and the objectives which the public corporations are set have to adjust accordingly.

One of the lessons learned from the regulation of the privatised utilities is that regulating prices and profits has to be supplemented with the setting and monitoring of quality of service measures. It has to be immediately recognised that the use of such measures is not without difficulties: the focus is on quantifiable rather than non-quantifiable aspects of the quality of service. And the manipulation of quality measures may occur – for example, to help meet arrival time targets, there is the incentive to lengthen the time-tabled journey time. But in the absence of measures, it becomes impossible to form any judgement about the quality of service.

The provision of unprofitable services leading to operating deficits which have to be covered by the government can involve what has been termed a 'soft budget constraint'. This general idea originated in the context of the Eastern European command economies and, although the terminology was not often used, this argument was influential in the push for privatisation. An enterprise can be said to face a soft budget constraint if it believes that in the event of costs exceeding revenue, it will have its deficit underwritten. Further, when a variety of subsidies are provided by government, the enterprise may pay more attention to lobbying for subsidies than to restraining costs or increasing revenue. This does not rule out subsidies where there are clear social gains from a public enterprise (or indeed a private enterprise) operating what would otherwise be an unprofitable activity. But it does suggest that subsidies should be provided in a transparent manner, and in return for delivering clearly specified benefits. It also suggests that subsidies should not be disguised in the accounts of the public enterprise through the cross-subsidisation of some consumers by others: provision of subsidies should be the responsibility of government and the tax payer rather than the consumer (though recognising that there is a substantial overlap between taxpayers and consumers).

The first conclusion we would draw from this discussion is that similar issues of level and structure of prices arise with public ownership as with regulated private ownership. Whilst recognising that there should be a link between price and cost, it also has to be said that the precise calculation of the cost of a particular service cannot be achieved when there are substantial fixed and joint costs. Further, public ownership permits that the structure of prices should also reflect distributional considerations. Perhaps most significantly, whilst public enterprise should be subject to financial targets and required to achieve a specified rate of return, it is also the case that the required rate of return is likely to be substantially lower than that required by the private sector.

The second conclusion is that clear objectives should be drawn up for public enterprises which in effect reflect the prevailing perception of the 'public interest'. What is seen to be the 'public interest' may well change over time, and the objectives of the public enterprise should be adjusted accordingly. Clarity of objectives aids the public monitoring and accountability of public enterprise, and the idea of community control is an important ingredient of the case for public ownership.

PERFORMANCE RELATED PAY

The massive pay increases awarded to the top echelons of managers have been one of the major scandals of privatisation. The payments to directors of private companies raise a wide range of issues which fall outside our remit, save to say that the salaries paid to managers in the private sector will have a strong influence on salaries which have to be paid to attract managers to work in the public sector. However, this raises the issue of the basis on which executive directors and other 'top' managers in a public enterprise should be rewarded, not only in terms of the level of their salaries and other benefits, but in terms of how their pay should be linked to performance indicators. 'Public firms are not, in theory, worse performers than private ones. But they must have properly designed incentive schemes for managers and workers' (de Fraja, 1995, p180).

Performance related pay by which pay is linked to general performance of the corporation (rather than to perceptions of the individual's performance) is often limited to executive directors of the corporation, even though the general performance is strongly dependent on the contributions of all workers and on the economic environment. In an era of rising profits and share prices, this form of performance related pay has generated large salaries for executive directors: but whether or not there has been any improvement in managerial performance is a moot point.

Seeking a salary structure which is relatively egalitarian faces some obvious difficulties in an era of increasing inequality. And yet, for many, one of the objectives of public ownership should be to make some contribution to a more egalitarian society. For the salary structure, an upper limit on the ratio of the income of the highest paid to the income of the lowest paid should be applied. In so far as performance related pay is used, it should be clear that performance is not solely the enhancement of the 'bottom line' but is more widely interpreted in terms of the 'public interest'. Further, in recognition of the collective causes of good performance, performance related pay should be more on a group basis than an individual one.

TRANSACTIONS COSTS AND VERTICAL INTEGRATION

The Conservative governments of the 1980s and 1990s pushed in many areas for the vertical disintegration of production. It was not always presented as vertical disintegration and went under a number of headings. The best known would probably be the contracting out of services from the public sector which had previously been undertaken by public sector workers – the contracting of cleaning services from the National Health Service, for example. It also had an impact in television with the imposed requirement that at least 25 per cent of programmes be made by companies other than the BBC or ITV. In the case of utilities vertical disintegration has frequently accompanied the process of privatisation. The apparent purpose of this press towards vertical disintegration was that it was part of a mechanism for introducing competition, whether to provide the contracted out service, to supply television programmes or to be a supplier of gas and electricity.

There is then a link between vertical integration and competition, namely that vertical integration of stages A and B within an enterprise in effect means that stage A is a monopoly supplier to stage B, and also of course that stage B is a monopsony purchaser from stage A. Part of the privatisation restructuring has been to separate those stages which are natural monopolies (e.g. distribution of electricity) from those stages which are potentially subject to competition (e.g. production of electricity). The process of vertical disintegration has allowed for the introduction of competition: for example competitive tendering for cleaning contracts. But it has also involved the substantial costs of competitive tendering, of ensuring quality of service, etc.

The idea of transactions costs is a relatively simple one, namely that there are costs associated with all transactions, whether those transactions take place through market exchange or within an organisation. Transactions costs have many facets and would include costs of search and negotiation, costs of specifying and monitoring a contract (governing a transaction) and costs of administration.

A set of ideas which has particularly influenced economists working on the economics of business and of industry, but which appears to have had no influence on British government policy, goes under the heading of 'transaction costs' (e.g. Williamson, 1985). Coase (1937) raised the question of why some economic activities are co-ordinated through the market whereas others are co-ordinated within organisations (notably for Coase firms, but also more generally organisations such as households or voluntary organisations). He contrasted the unconscious co-ordination of the market with the conscious co-ordination of the organisation: Alfred Chandler was later to contrast the invisible hand (of the market) with the visible hand (of administration). Williamson developed Coase's idea that there are costs associated with using the market (transaction costs), and that an organisation can compare the costs of buying an input from other firms with the costs of producing that input for itself. The costs to one firm of buying from another firm include not only the price which is paid for the input but the costs of searching for prospective suppliers, negotiating prices etc. But transaction costs involve much more than the costs of search, and include matters such as ensuring the quality of what is produced and reducing the risk of being exploited by the other party's opportunism.

Another way of expressing this idea is to say that economic relationships are governed by contracts, which may be explicit and/or implicit, and the terms may be specific to that contract and/or incorporate general presumptions of the common law. But contracts may be complicated to write and difficult to monitor and enforce. Many contracts, of which employment contracts are a notable example, are often imprecise and leave much room for discretion on both sides. It would not be feasible to write (or even think of) a fully specified contract which dictated what was to be done in every conceivable situation (and many situations may be inconceivable). Contracts, whether employment or intra-firm, raise principal-agent issues, that is the degree to which one party to the contract (the principal) can ensure that the other party (the agent) operates in ways which the principal would wish. There are many instances when the writing and monitoring of contracts within a firm are less difficult and costly compared with equivalent contracts between one firm and another firm or set of firms.

These ideas have obvious significance for issues such as contracting out within the public sector. The writing and monitoring of contracts issued by the public authority to private companies has been a major problem in many instances of contracting out, notably over the quality of the service provided.

Vertical disintegration has been undertaken in pursuit of competition, though how long that competition will last before consolidation sets in – through acquisitions for example – is an important question. Vertical disintegration has generated substantial transactions costs: that is, a company at one stage of the production process has to contract with one at the subsequent stage. Train operators have to contract with Railtrack, for example. This vertical disintegration does raise significant questions for any proposals for public ownership: for example, should a complete industry be taken into public ownership and re-integrated, or should competition in an industry be maintained between publicly owned and privately owned companies, or between a number of publicly owned companies?

PUBLIC OWNERSHIP AND DEMOCRATIC PARTICIPATION

Two conflicting considerations might arise with democratic participation in public enterprises. On the one hand, we want public enterprise to be managed in an effective and innovative manner, with managers and workers using their skills, talents and professional judgement to best effect. This would entail managers and workers 'getting on with the job' without external interference and meddling, and would allow them to develop the public enterprise. On the other hand, we would intend that public ownership should involve a degree of democratic control: the purpose of public ownership is ultimately to have an accountable and effective operation. Many of the objectives of public ownership elaborated in Chapter 2 relate to community control and involvement.

The usual way in which these conflicting considerations are reconciled is that day-to-day decisions (the tactics) of the public enterprise are the responsibility of managers whilst the framework (the strategy) within which they operate is laid down by government. As indicated in a previous section there was some tendency towards tightening the operational framework during the forty or so years of nationalisation, from a broad requirement to pursue the public interest to the setting of target rates of return and imposing external financing limits. Thus one element of accountability of the public corporation may be secured through monitoring the implementation of its agreed overall strategy. But another element would be a more local accountability, which requires some framework of local groups which are able to monitor and influence the more immediate activities of the public corporation.

AGENCY PROBLEMS

The general problem of agency is how to ensure that the intentions of one group (often called the 'principals') are carried out by another group (often called 'agents') when the principals have hired the agents to act on their behalf. This is such a ubiquitous situation that we may not give a great deal of thought to its implications, especially in the context of public ownership. The situation of regulated privatised utilities involves a range of principal-agent problems: owners of the utility hire managers, government hires the regulators, regulators oversee managers of the privatised utility. At each stage there are difficulties in the principal (e.g. the government) ensuring that the agent (the regulators) act as the principal would wish.

Under public ownership, nationalised industries had a sponsoring ministry and were to some degree subject to scrutiny by that ministry and by Parliament through the Select Committee on Nationalised Industries. Nationalised industries were subject to various performance targets (such as the requirement to break even in the first two decades or so and, more recently, rate-of-return targets) but also at times their prices would be constrained in the pursuit of counter-inflation policies. Since privatisation, scrutiny has passed to the office of the regulators, and prices have been controlled by RPI – x type formulae. The system under nationalisation and that under privatisation both run the danger of 'agency capture', when the body which should be acting on behalf of the public, to ensure that the enterprise or industry is operated in an efficient and responsible manner, comes to act more on behalf of the enterprise or industry. Under nationalisation, the sponsoring ministry may act more as the industry's champion within government, whilst under privatisation the regulatory body may come to reflect the producers' interests.

The problem of agency is a complex one and we will not attempt to solve it here. But we will make some remarks on its implications in the context of the utilities and public ownership. First, perhaps surprisingly, public ownership may involve fewer agency problems (or at least fewer layers of principal-agent relationship) than regulated private ownership. Simply, regulated private ownership introduces the layer between government and regulator and regulator and utility as compared with public ownership. Second, there is a degree of monitoring of privatised utilities through regulatory bodies, and the specification of a range of performance indicators. This type of monitoring entails costs and has its own problems. Nevertheless, it does involve a degree of scrutiny over the performance of the utilities.

CONCLUDING REMARKS

This chapter has had two purposes. First we examined some of the objections raised against public ownership, especially in terms of their alleged inefficiencies. We argued that, on both empirical and theoretical grounds, public ownership does not necessarily involve any more inefficiency than private ownership does. But some structures and organisations of public corporations are likely to be more effective than others. The monolithic nationalised industries established by the Attlee government were much influenced by the perceived benefits of economies of scale, vertical integration and rationalisation. This led into the second purpose of the chapter, which was to elaborate on some considerations about how public corporations might be structured and organised.

7

OPTIONS FOR PUBLIC OWNERSHIP

INTRODUCTION

The purpose of this chapter is to consider a range of options for the form of public ownership. The model which is often invoked when public ownership is discussed is that of the nationalised industries, as largely put into place by the 1945-51 Labour governments. These were mainly established as monopolies (in the strict sense of the word) protected from competition and with little or no involvement of workers or consumers in the management or decision-making processes. In our consideration of the various options, it is acknowledged that this form of nationalisation may not be the most desirable and may (through changes in technology, in ideas) no longer be particularly appropriate.

The range of options which we examine starts from the list proposed by UNISON, which is as follows:

(i) full public ownership (or nationalisation), which would involve 100 per cent ownership and a (re)integrated industry, akin in many cases to that undertaken by the post-war Labour government and to the pre-privatisation position;
(ii) partial public ownership, with the government taking a substantial stake in the utilities: this option can be subdivided into majority ownership and minority ownership;
(iii) strategic public ownership, achieved by nationalising key parts of the utilities such as the National Grid;
(iv) regional ownership, achieved by constitutional bodies such as the Scottish Parliament, the Welsh Assembly or Regional Government taking an ownership stake in the utilities operating within their areas;
(v) mutualisation, under which consumers become the collective owners of the utility companies;

(vi) democratic employee ownership, using different methods of democratic control to achieve common ownership.

We now discuss these alternative models in turn, seeking to indicate how each model might work and noting the advantages and disadvantages of each. It should be said that there is no presumption here that there is a unique best (or worst) model for public ownership, and in general the different natures of the industries means that while one model may be appropriate for industry X, another may be more appropriate for industry Y. We also recognise that some options are more politically feasible than others. We will return to this issue in the next chapter where we discuss how well each option would match the requirements of the various utilities.

All of the options considered face a set of similar obstacles, which have been discussed in Chapter 5: the perceived costs of public ownership, legal constraints, parliamentary time and the existing structures of the industries. We do not repeat that discussion here, though we would expect that, while none of those obstacles is insurmountable, some of the options may face more obstacles than others. Additionally we would note that options such as regional public ownership would require the construction of corresponding public authorities (in England) to own and monitor the public enterprises.

FULL PUBLIC OWNERSHIP

The Morrisonian form of public ownership was the model followed for the railways, coal industry, gas, electricity, and from the late 1960s onwards postal services and telecommunications. This form had some key characteristics. Firstly, the industry (which was relatively easy to define) was operated as a single vertically integrated enterprise (with the exception of electricity where there was a separation between the Central Electricity Generating Board, CEGB, and regional electricity boards). With the partial exception of British Rail, which continued to operate hotels and ferries previously operated by the pre-nationalisation rail companies, the nationalised companies were limited to what would now be termed their core business. Secondly, the nationalised company was a statutory monopoly and private companies were not permitted to provide the goods or services concerned (there were partial exceptions to this, e.g. small coal mines could be operated, Hull Council had (and still has) its own telephone company).

This model was followed in some respects by later extensions of public ownership (steel in the 1960s, shipbuilding, aircraft production in the 1970s) with the formation of a single state-owned nationalised company. However, the 1970s nationalisations differed in that the British industries were in competition with foreign industries, and were not given protected monopoly position (that is other companies could be established to produce steel, ships, aircraft).

The full public ownership option differs from those considered below in some important respects, namely that the industry under public ownership would be operated on a vertically integrated basis, and on a national basis. The enterprise could be run on a divisional basis (with the divisions organised along regional and/or functional lines), but those would be divisions of a single enterprise. As such the single enterprise would be owned by national government and the enterprise as a whole would be accountable to Parliament. The full public ownership option (as defined here) would exclude the possibility of regional accountability and is also taken to exclude the competitive provision of part of the industry (e.g. electricity generation in the electricity industry).

The option described as full public ownership would entail the nationalised industry being a vertically integrated enterprise, but being excluded from provision of goods and services outside of its remit. This would enable the nationalised companies to focus on their core business, which in the case of the utilities is the provision of gas, electricity and water to the British public. It would generally preclude overseas operations, other than those which are necessary for the provision of services within the UK. Vertical integration can bring benefits in terms of coordination between different stages of production, and reduce the transactions and contractual costs involved in vertical disintegration, as has been discussed in Chapter 6.

Full public ownership would in effect require the nationalisation of the whole of the industry (whether gas, electricity or water). This would entail the compulsory public acquisition of the assets and resources employed in the provision of those services. This compulsory acquisition raises some difficulties, which we will shortly discuss. Previous nationalisations have faced similar difficulties, and hence they cannot be insurmountable. Similar problems arise with most of the other options we consider below in so far as they would entail compulsory acquisition of assets.

The first problem arises from the observation that privatised utilities have diversified outside of the core business which they inherited on privatisation. This includes diversification in terms of product range and of areas of operation. The second complication arises from the emergence of companies other than the privatised utilities who are now involved in the gas and electricity industries, notably in the production of gas and electricity. A third obstacle is the acquisition of privatised utilities by other companies.

The discussion in Chapter 5 has indicated that diversification, emergence of new producers and acquisition of utilities means that the framework of and legislation for public ownership becomes much more complex. It would require either that the assets to be acquired be specified in the legislation or more likely that the companies to be acquired would be specified, followed by divestiture after nationalisation of those parts of the business which are not central to the provision of gas, electricity or water. The production and supply of gas and electricity by a range of companies leads to the question of how far the facilities for that production and supply would be taken into public ownership or, if left in private ownership, the terms on which those facilities produce and supply gas and electricity which is distributed by the nationalised industries. It also raises the question of the restrictions which would be placed on the future production and supply of electricity and gas outside of the nationalised industries. Prior to privatisation there were limits placed on the generation of electricity for own consumption and for supply to others.

Privatised utilities operating as subsidiaries of other companies should, in principle, be 'ring fenced' for the purposes of regulation. Thus public ownership would involve the compulsory acquisition of these 'ring fenced' subsidiaries. The only novel feature which would arise here (as compared with previous nationalisations) is that this would involve in a number of cases the nationalisation of assets owned by foreign companies, which would be particularly so in the case of the regional electricity companies.

The nationalised industry would operate as a vertically integrated statutory monopoly (at least over parts of its operation such as distribution). It has been usual Treasury practice to consolidate the borrowing requirements of the nationalised industries into the government budget. Hence, any borrowing to finance investment undertaken by the nationalised industry is regarded as adding to the public sector borrowing requirement (PSBR). The net effect on the PSBR depends on the balance between the flow of profits of the nationalised utility and its investment financing requirements.

The statutory monopoly aspect of the nationalised utility requires that mechanisms be put in place to ensure that the utility is answerable to both government and consumers. The government must lay down the broad parameters within which the nationalised utility operates: in other words, if the nationalised utility is to benefit the 'public interest', that interest has to be specified. This specification may be in terms of pricing structure, investment policy, universal supply obligation etc., but needs to be undertaken in a clear manner (*cf* previous discussion in Chapter 6). The monopoly element of the nationalised utility also requires mechanisms (such as performance indicators, consumer representative groups) to ensure that there is no monopoly exploitation of the consumer: such monopoly exploitation could take the form of slovenly service, or poor reliability, as much as high prices.

PARTIAL PUBLIC OWNERSHIP

Partial public ownership could cover the range from government owning an insignificant proportion of a company through to owning virtually all of it. The figures quoted in Chapter 2 indicate that government retains a small ownership stake in the privatised utilities. There have been previous examples of much more extensive, though partial, ownership of companies: the best known are probably the 51 per cent stake in BP and the around 95 per cent stake in British Leyland. As the last example illustrates, partial public ownership has often come about through the rescue of privately owned companies in distress.

The proportion of a company owned by the government under partial public ownership is relevant for the exercise of control by government (if that is the objective): without control, government acts as a rentier in the company concerned, passively receiving dividends. The example of BP illustrates that even when government could exercise some control over a company (in that it held around half of the shares of the company), it does not necessarily do so. Under partial public ownership, the company involved would remain a private corporation in which the government happens to be a major shareholder. As with any other shareholder, government's ability to exercise control would depend on its voting power relative to that of other shareholders, and its willingness to appoint directors and to intervene as a shareholder in the management of the company.

Partial public ownership can be achieved through the simple device of government purchasing shares in the company concerned. We have remarked above that there is a degree of minority public ownership already: as the figures quoted in Chapter 2 reveal, the government has a (very) small stake in a number of privatised utilities, with local government through their pension funds having a more significant stake. But these shares are generally held in an essentially passive manner, with the relevant tier of government receiving dividends but playing no active role in the management of the company. Further, trustees of local authority pension funds would be constrained to seek the highest rate of return for the funds. However, the pooling and coordination of these share holdings would be equivalent to minority public ownership, albeit on a modest scale. Through these share holdings the public sector could exert some leverage on the private companies if it were so minded.

Partial public ownership has the attraction that it does not require the complex legislation which complete public ownership would require. In this context 'complete public ownership' means any of the other forms of public ownership considered here, as they would each require the compulsory acquisition of privately owned assets. But this route to partial public ownership would require the government to buy shares in the open market. Once it became clear (or was announced policy) that the government was acquiring shares in a company, that company's share prices could be expected to rise. Evidence on acquisitions would suggest that a premium over the initial share price of the order of 25 per cent may have to be paid to acquire a substantial slice of shares in a company. There are generally limits, under the Take-over Code, on the extent to which one company can buy up shares in another without making a formal take-over bid and hence buying all the shares in that company. It is then debatable whether or not the government could acquire, say, 40 per cent of a company's shares without having to make a take-over bid for it. This would not necessarily be a legal requirement, but may be seen as reasonable in comparison with the requirements laid on private companies.

Minority public ownership would not involve control. It would enable the government to act like any other large shareholder. In concert with other large shareholders, it might, for example, be able to change senior management. But minority public ownership (as the BP example indicates) is little more than the state acting as a rentier, receiving dividends from the company but having little other involvement with it.

Partial public ownership as envisaged here is the partial ownership of a parent company, and cannot be applied to the partial ownership of companies which are currently subsidiaries of other concerns. Almost all of the regional electricity companies are now wholly owned subsidiaries of other companies. In some cases the parent company is another utility, and hence no particular problems would arise. But in other cases, the parent company is a foreign-based company, of which the REC is a wholly owned subsidiary. In such a case, partial public ownership of the REC would not be possible through purchase of shares on the open market. It is (just) possible that the foreign-based company would agree to state involvement in the REC if sufficient leverage could be applied (e.g. through bargaining over the conditions of the license to distribute electricity), but this does seem a rather far fetched scenario.

Partial public ownership means that the company concerned remains a separate entity and is not regarded as a part of the state. The government is a major shareholder but there is an 'arms-length' relationship between the company and the state, which acts rather like any other large shareholder, such as a financial institution. While the government receives dividends from the company (which form part of the revenue of the government), there is no sense in which the company's accounts are consolidated with those of the government. Hence when the company borrows, it does so on its own account and on the basis of its own credit rating. This may well mean that it borrows at somewhat higher interest rates than the government would be able to do, but it also means that any borrowing is not regarded as part of the public sector borrowing requirement (PSBR).

Public ownership can be viewed as an alternative mechanism for the regulation of natural monopolies. However, partial public ownership would not give government or Parliament the control over the company which would come from complete public ownership (whether organised on a national, regional or local basis). Thus, partial public ownership of companies in a natural monopoly position would still require that there was some regulation, very much as at present. Partial public ownership also means that the company in which the government acquires a stake remains a private company, subject to the range of company law and with obligations to its shareholders, whether government, individuals or institutions. This would severely limit the extent to which the company could be operated in the 'public interest' when the pursuit of that interest conflicts with profitability.

STRATEGIC PUBLIC OWNERSHIP

Strategic public ownership would involve the public ownership of some key elements within an industry or within the economy. In the case of the utilities, this would mean the public ownership of the basic network. It would involve, for example, public ownership of the national grid in the electricity industry or of the rail track in the case of the railways. The national grid and the rail track are strategic in the sense that they are cases of natural monopoly and are the key networks for the electricity and rail industries respectively. In the vertically-disintegrated industries of electricity, gas and the railways, it is clearly feasible for key elements of those industries to be brought back into public ownership, while other parts remain under private ownership or some mixture of public and private ownership. For example, in the case of electricity, national and local distribution of electricity constitute natural monopolies whereas electricity supply can be undertaken by a larger number of firms under competitive conditions.

The network is the key element in most of the utilities, and is the part of the system where the position of natural monopoly arises. Further, there is often concern over the safety of the network and over who can have access to it. Thus in the case of the railways, there is concern that track, signalling, etc, meet safety requirements, and that trains are operated in a safe manner.

Insofar as strategic public ownership can arise in vertically disintegrated industries with public ownership of key parts of the industry, it faces the same costs and problems of vertical disintegration as does the present industrial structure. When different bodies operate different parts of the system, there have to be contractual and other relationships between them. The writing and enforcement of contracts can be costly. Disputes can readily arise when there are problems: in the case of a rail accident, how is responsibility to be allocated ? There are problems of coordination of investment plans as are currently arising in the railway industry. These problems do not entirely disappear in a vertically integrated industry, but they become a matter for internal resolution.

In other respects, strategic public ownership faces many of the same issues as full public ownership: indeed it is complete public ownership but of only a part of the industry. But there are some differences, in that the companies currently providing network services (e.g. national grid, Railtrack) are themselves non-diversified monopolies, and hence issues of diversification and competition do not arise.

REGIONAL PUBLIC OWNERSHIP

In this section we discuss two different forms of regional public ownership. The first, which for convenience we will refer to as regional public ownership, refers to the establishment of publicly owned companies at a sub-national level, which operate as a statutory monopoly, as could be the case with the distribution of electricity or water. The second, which we will refer to as 'local authority ownership', refers to the establishment of publicly owned companies, again at the sub-national level, which operate in competition with other companies, whether publicly or privately owned and whether or not located in the same area. An emerging example here would be the involvement of local authorities in the production of electricity. Ownership in this context involves the receipt of any operating surpluses and the underwriting of any deficits (though that would presumably be subject to limits imposed by the European Union on state assistance for enterprises).

Although there are some common issues and themes which arise for regional public ownership and local government public ownership, there are also some significant differences, and we treat them in sequence. There are also intermediate options which would mirror in some ways arrangements for fire and other services, that is a grouping of a number of local authorities.

(i) regional public ownership

The water and electricity industries have long been structured on a regional basis. But prior to privatisation, the ownership of regional electricity boards and the water companies lay with national government, and the boards and companies were answerable to the relevant government minister and to Parliament. What we are discussing here would be rather different in that ownership, control and accountability would lie at the regional level. The regional authority in which ownership was vested could be regional government. While there is no regional government at present, within the next few years there will be a Scottish Parliament, Assemblies in Wales and Northern Ireland, and the election of a Mayor and Assembly in London, which will bring regional government over a significant part of the United Kingdom. We will continue to refer to regional ownership in this discussion, even though in the cases just cited it would actually be national ownership in the devolved nations. In the absence of regional government in the rest of the UK, the regional authority in which ownership is vested could be a specifically created body, based on the local authorities in the areas concerned, or the existing civil service based regional executives.

Regional public ownership could arise through a number of different routes. A recent report by UNISON (1996) refers to 'constitutional bodies such as a Scottish Parliament, Welsh Assembly or Regional Government in England, making a bid for, or taking a stake in, the utilities within their areas'. Seeking to make an acquisition on a voluntary basis (so far as the shareholders of the utility are concerned) faces some significant difficulties, similar to those discussed above in the context of partial public ownership. Acquisitions usually require the payment of a significant premium over the market share price (often of the order of 25 to 30 per cent). In those cases where regionally based companies (e.g. the Regional Electricity Companies and the Water Companies) have been acquired by other companies (whether UK or overseas based), such an acquisition becomes more difficult (though not ruled out in the event that the parent company is willing to sell the utility subsidiary). There are also complications arising from the lack of coincidence between the boundaries of a region (or collection of local authorities) and those of the operations of the utility. The building up of a stake at the regional level parallels, in a number of respects, the partial public ownership at the national level. This has been discussed above.

The purchase of a utility by regional government or authority does not raise financing issues additional to those discussed in Chapter 5. The regional government could issue bonds, either in its own name or that of the acquired utility, and finance the acquisition from the proceeds. Depending on which regional authority, and the financial power given to it by central government, a bond issue might well require permission by central government.

In the event that regions were able to determine whether or not there was public ownership of a utility in their area, it is likely that there would be variations across the country, with some regions opting for public ownership and others not. This would mean that the regulatory framework would have to remain, at least to cover those remaining privately owned. But it would clearly be possible for the regulatory functions to be carried out at the regional level (which is the case in the United States where regulation is applied at the state level).

While many considerations regarding regional public ownership parallel those regarding national public ownership, there is also the need to determine in which government body ownership of the public enterprise would be lodged. That body would receive any surplus generated and would be responsible for any deficit, and would be the one to which the managers of the public enterprise would be answerable; it would be the one through which democratic accountability would be exercised. As indicated above, the relevant tier of government will soon be clear-cut outside of England, but would pose some difficulties in England in the absence of regional government.

If and when regional government is established in England, there would be a decisive argument for mapping the geographical scope of the public enterprise with the regional government. There would then be an obvious and close relationship between the public enterprise and the regional Parliament and government, with the public enterprise accountable to the regional Parliament. With the establishment of the Scottish Parliament, and the Welsh and Northern Ireland Assemblies, there would be a clear opportunity for ownership and control over regional publicly owned enterprises to rest with those institutions. In England, in the absence of regional government, regional public ownership would require the establishment of regional bodies which would oversee the regional enterprises. These bodies may be consortiums of local authorities, similar to those established to cover the metropolitan areas for a range of functions. In a recent White Paper (*Building Partnerships for Prosperity*) the government proposed the creation of a Regional Development Agency (RDA) in each region 'to promote sustainable economic development and social and physical regeneration and to co-ordinate the work of regional and local partners in areas such as training, investment, regeneration and business support'. The RDAs would be established as 'Government-sponsored public bodies which are business-led and which reflect the perspectives and needs of each region and the main interest groups within each region'. Although ownership would be lodged with the national government, it would clearly be possibile for control and accountability over regional public corporations to lie with the proposed RDAs.

There is also, however, an argument that the boundaries of the area of operation of a public enterprise should depend on geography and demography. As the population size and geographical scope of the area covered by a local authority vary according to a range of considerations, so could the scope of public enterprise. For many of the services being considered (e.g. provision of gas, electricity), distribution is to individual use points (e.g. homes, factories) and it is the nature of the distribution network to generate a situation of natural monopoly. That is, there would be needless duplication with more than one distribution network. But this observation of the natural monopoly features of the distribution network says nothing about how large an area (a geographical area if distance is important or an economic one if the volume of services provided by a single supplier is important) should be covered by a single supplier. For example, it does not indicate whether electricity distribution should be organised at a local, regional or national level (or some intermediate one).

From a cost perspective there may be economies of scale in the generation of electricity, and if the generation of electricity is closely linked with its distribution this would lead to a minimum practical size for an electricity company. But the economies of scale in electricity production are unlikely to be such as to require a minimum size covering a population of more than, say, 100,000. There may also be some economies of scale in certain activities, such as billing, which serves to place a floor under the size of an electricity distribution company (although if such economies of scale were at all significant, joint ventures for, say, billing could be established by a consortium of electricity distribution companies).

There is also the consideration of variation in demand. This is, in effect, the argument for a national grid so that high levels of demand in one area can be met by supply from other areas, so avoiding the necessity of each area having sufficient capacity to meet peak demand. The significance of these remarks is that there would appear to be no imperative from the cost side for gas, electricity and water distribution to be organised on a regional or national basis, provided that (especially in the case of electricity) there are mechanisms for the transfer of gas, electricity or water from area to area to meet variations in demand. Then a political judgement would need to be made regarding the organisational relationship between the utilities and the political structure. For example, the general absence of regional government in the UK might limit the possibilities for democratic involvement with utilities.

There is no necessity for uniformity of organisation across the country. Indeed at present there are significant differences in ownership of the water industry between Scotland and the rest of Britain. A lack of uniformity could arise from some regions opting for public ownership while others opt for private ownership. Another dimension of a lack of uniformity might arise in respect of the geographical scope of public enterprise: it might be appropriate in some cases for the geographical scope of the public enterprise to be equivalent to a metropolitan area (such as West Yorkshire) and in other cases to be a region. These are essentially practical matters which could be settled by reference to the extent of economies of scale and of scope and to the geographical and demographic features of the area.

(ii) local authority public ownership

Although it may now be almost forgotten, there was a long and substantial involvement of local authorities in the provision of gas and electricity before nationalisation in the 1940s. Local authorities are, though, likely to be too small (in terms of population and consumption of the utilities services) for organisation of the utilities to be at local authority level. This would, however not preclude a grouping of local authorities (at say the level of the abolished metropolitan counties) being an efficient size for the organisation of some utilities.

In an environment in which gas and electricity supply is undertaken on a competitive basis (whether under public or private ownership), there would be no reason to exclude local authorities from participating in the ownership and management of supply facilities. Indeed there would be reason for encouraging them to participate. This might well require central government authority to secure the necessary finance.

A particular issue which does arise in the case of competitive local government public ownership is the degree of coincidence between the geographical area of operation of the local public enterprise and the area covered by the local authority.

MUTUALISATION

Mutualisation means that the company is owned in some collective sense by its customers, at least in the sense that some share of the company's operating surplus accrues to the customers. There is no individual ownership by customers or members, though there can be payment (of part of the surplus) to individuals, usually on the basis of their custom (the retail co-operatives being the clearest example of this with the payment of the 'divi'). Mutualisation has been suggested by some, particularly for the water industry since everyone is a consumer of water, and the members of the mutual organisation (the customers) would be coincident with the general population (see, for example, Holtham, 1996).

There has been considerable experience of mutual organisations:

building societies, retail co-operatives, mutual life assurance companies, AA and RAC, and (prior to its privatisation) the TSB. These mutual organisations have generally concentrated their business in their core activity and have not usually diversified. Some would argue that concentration on a core business has brought gains in terms of effectiveness. It can also be noted that mutuals have operated successfully as utilities in the United States though, as Morse (1997) states, under a variety of names such as co-operatives or rural water districts. These have been mutual organisations in that ownership rights rest with the utility's customers (who cannot in these cases sell or transfer those ownership rights).

There are questions of how democratic these mutual organisations have been and how much influence their members have on their operations. There is the danger that customers have no influence over the management and decision-making of the mutual organisation and that the management becomes self-perpetuating. Thus there is the requirement for any mutual organisation involved in the utilities to have an organisational framework within which customers can influence the decisions of their organisation.

There are many examples of successful mutual organisations, at least in the sense that they have survived and prospered. Judging from that, the mutual organisation is a feasible option for the utilities. It is also the case that the comparative performance of these organisations (that is compared with capitalist companies) has generally been good.

Mutual organisations generate two types of problem (and these are echoed in the case of worker co-operatives as discussed in the next section). The first is that their rate of investment (and hence their rate of growth) is limited by the available finance, which comes from their own operating surplus. Mutual organisations typically finance their own expansion (as indeed do many privately owned corporations). This self-financing is not inevitable but it is likely that financial markets will be reluctant to lend to them. In the case of an organisation financing its investment internally out of its surplus, if, for example, the operating surplus were equivalent to 10 per cent of sales, the maximum level of investment would also be equivalent to 10 per cent of sales. Since investment is required for the growth, this places a limit on the rate of expansion of the mutual organisation.

The second problem arises from the observation that, as the mutual organisation grows over time, it accrues capital assets which are owned by it in a collective sense and hence by the members collectively. There may be a considerable surplus accrued by the mutual organisation, which can be 'unlocked' by the current members if the organisation demutualises, as evidenced by the recent changes of many building societies into privately owned companies. Current members are then in effect receiving the 'enforced' savings of previous members: in the case of building societies the surpluses had been accumulated over a century or more. Those surpluses were money which could potentially have been returned to earlier generations of members, but was instead used to finance the expansion of the activities of the organisation.

Mutualisation would require the re-acquisition of the now privatised company, probably by the government, and then its handing over to the company's customers. It is possible to conceive of a compulsory capital levy on customers, though that raises several different questions. To what extent would customers have the available capital? On what basis would the levy be made (e.g. on the basis of a fixed sum for each household, varying by number of members of the household or by consumption level)? Regarding the former, it can be noted that the stock market valuation of the water companies is, at the time of writing, of the order of £25 to £30 billion (*cf* Chapter 5), which is equivalent to around £1,000 per household or water company customer. However, an alternative would be possible whereby the government acquires the privatised company on behalf of the customers, and then charges interest on the capital cost of acquisition. Hence the dividends received by the customers would be the company's operating surplus minus investment expenditure minus interest payments, assuming that the company finances its own investment instead of borrowing.

The customers of the mutual organisation are also its owners, and the board of directors is then elected by the customer-owners. The customer becomes a member by virtue of being a customer and, in general, voting is on a one person (customer) one vote basis (though variations are possible). But the concept of a mutual organisation (as of a workers' co-operative) is essentially based on membership which implies one person one vote. It should be noted that this would imply that large users (especially businesses) have the same voting rights as small users.

Mutualisation offers a range of advantages. Firstly, there is payment of dividends to customers, which would give them a 'double interest' in the company and its efficient operation – as customers and as owners. The question then arises as to the mechanisms through which the customers and owners can express their interests to ensure efficient operations. This problem is not a great deal different from that faced by the shareholders of large corporations who have very limited ability, or incentive, to influence the operation of a company. We have cast doubt, in a previous chapter, on the efficacy of the take-over threat as a mechanism by which shareholders (potential and actual) can influence managers and ensure efficient operation of the company. But clearly in the case of a mutual company, there can be no take-over threat (more accurately no take-over threat compatible with the survival of the mutual form: examples from building societies show that privately owned companies can take over mutuals, as in the case of Lloyd Bank's acquisition of the Cheltenham and Gloucester Building Society).

Another advantage might be an identification between the company and its operations and the people of the region which it serves. The company is owned by and responsible to its customers. There is no prospect of the company 'upping sticks' and moving elsewhere. Also, the mutual organisation can provide a form of regional autonomy which does not rely on the creation of regional government, and can operate outside the regional political process.

Finally, although it is not an inevitable feature of a mutual company, it is likely that the company would limit its operations to the region and to a single product (e.g. water, electricity as the case may be). This has been the pattern with most existing mutual companies, and it could be made a legally binding constraint (in recognition of the privileges which a mutual company with a monopoly position would have). But it may be something which the owners of the company would in any case wish to accept.

Some other points arise regarding the mutual organisation which would have to be resolved. First is the question of who are to be treated as customers and, more significantly the ways in which the interests of different types of customer are to be protected and reconciled. It may be self-evident who are customers and, at least with water and electricity, it is likely that all households and businesses would be customers. But it is possible, depending on the precise legislation, that some electricity users would be able to generate their own electricity and not be customers of the mutualised utility. However the general structure of utility pricing is for a standing charge and a charge based on use, and there is often some difference in the level and structure of charges for private households and for businesses.

The second point is the basis on which the dividend would be paid.

It could be paid on a *per capita* basis so that everyone (or at least each household) would receive the same dividend. An alternative, and most likely, would be to base the dividend on some measure of use.

Third, there may still be issues of how to regulate the operations of the organisation. It could be argued that a mutual company would not require to be regulated over price, since if it were to charge an 'excessive' price and earn 'excessive' profits, those profits would be paid back to the customers as a dividend in their role as the company's collective owners. Further, if dividends were paid proportional to usage, the effective price paid by a customer would be lower than the actual price by the dividend. In the case of a statutory monopoly, there may still be a need for regulation: for example on rules governing disconnection and rights to universal service. It can be noted that American utility mutuals are either not subject to regulation over their prices and profits or subject to a streamlined system of approval (Morse, 1997).

Fourth, the mutual organisation should be embedded into a democratic structure in which the organisation is answerable to its customer-owners. A minimum requirement would be that the board of directors is elected by and answerable to the customer-owners. It would also be assumed that there would be trade union recognition.

The extensive experience of mutual organisations should show that the mutual form is a viable option. The demise of some mutual organisations (e.g. many former building societies) has emanated from the financial gains which can be made by members on de-mutualisation. This in effect secures for current members the accumulated reserves of the mutual company, which in turn are based on the foregone earnings of members in the past. This route would in effect be ruled out by legislation which tied together the company's mutual status with its statutory rights and obligations. As ever, what Parliament does, a future Parliament can undo: but the de-mutualisation would require an Act of Parliament.

DEMOCRATIC EMPLOYEE OWNERSHIP

A workers' co-operative is a form of social ownership which could operate at local, regional or national level. Thus workers' co-operatives (and indeed mutual organisations) could be combined with, for example, regional organisation. Indeed it could be argued that workers' co-operatives operate more successfully (in terms of genuine worker involvement in decision-making) on a smaller scale rather than on a larger one.

The key attribute of a workers' co-operative is that the workers are the collective owners of the enterprise and as such have title to its net revenue. Its net revenue is the difference between the receipts of the enterprise and its costs (of materials and, if relevant, interest charges). The revenue is divided into workers' wages, retained surplus to be used to finance investment in capital equipment, and the workers' dividend. In workers' co-operatives, the main distinction between wages and the workers' dividend is that the former is usually paid on a regular basis (weekly or monthly typically), whereas the latter is paid after the year end, and is dependent on the co-op's performance and fortunes during that year. However the division between wages and dividend is a matter of convenience for the workers since both payments are made to themselves.

One of the key decisions for the workers to make collectively is how to divide their co-operative's net revenue between immediate income for themselves (wages plus workers dividend) and investment in capital expenditure and expansion which is intended to provide additional income in the future. The basis on which that surplus is shared out among the workers varies. It may be proportional to their wage, it may be proportional to their own capital stake in the co-operative, it may be on a per capita basis. Other variants and mixtures of variants are possible.

Workers' co-operatives are organised in many different ways, but for our purposes two features of their organisation are particularly relevant. First, there is the question of financing. In the context of a workers' co-operative there are only two alternatives. These are borrowing on a non-equity basis (e.g. through loans or bonds whether at fixed or variable interest rates) or use of the workers' own funds (whether through explicit provision of funds by the workers or, more usually, through the retention of part of the revenue of the co-operative). If finance were to be provided on an equity (i.e. profit-sharing) basis by non-workers it would mean that 'outsiders (other than workers) would have some title to the surplus of the enterprise and by definition the enterprise would no longer be a workers' co-operative.

Second, there is the extent of internal democracy and participation. Formal control of a workers' co-operative rests with the workers, usually on the basis of one worker one vote. In place of the board of directors elected by shareholders in a capitalist firm, there can be the elections of directors by the workers. The control by shareholders over the board of directors and over the managers of the company can often be nominal in capitalist firms, and effective control of the company lies with the top level of management. However, a similar situation can easily occur in workers' co-operatives with effective control passing to the higher echelons of management and with little or no worker involvement. A workers' co-operative in the utilities would be a relatively large organisation, and the effective participation of workers in that context can be problematic. A trade union in a workers' co-operative appears at first sight contradictory: it involves workers organising to bargain with themselves. However, in a large workers' co-operative, which those established in utilities would be, there would be a continuing need for workers to be represented in negotiations with management, even when management has been elected by the workers.

Workers' co-operatives face two sets of difficulties relating to finance. First, it is often observed that there is a reluctance on the part of financial institutions to lend to workers' co-operatives. Clearly the equity source of finance is ruled out; hence finance has to be raised either from the retained surpluses of the workers' co-operative or through borrowing at pre-determined interest rates.

Second, it is often argued that there might be reluctance on the part of the current work-force to undertake investment financed out of the revenue of the co-operative. The key argument can be represented as follows: suppose that a workers' co-operative is seeking to decide whether to make a £1 million investment decision or to pay the £1 million out as dividend to the current workers. The investment will, with luck, bring future revenue to the co-operative, spread over the lifetime of that investment. It might generate employment in the co-operative, in which case membership expands, and the future revenue is shared out by a greater number of people. It might raise productivity of the current workforce, thereby raising their own future income. Current members who may be contemplating retirement or leaving the co-operative for other reasons (more especially if leaving in the near future, but to some degree over the lifetime of the investment project) are likely to prefer the dividend now to uncertain future gains for the co-operative, which in any event will not directly benefit them. Even for members who intend to remain with the co-operative, there might be a reluctance to vote for the investment, which involves some risk, and the benefits of which might largely accrue to new members who join to work on the new investment.

This perceived reluctance to invest, which would tend to hold back the expansion of the co-operative, and might lead to a relatively labour-intensive mode of production, could be alleviated through a combination of two possibilities. These are for the co-operative to draw on external borrowing on a non-equity basis (i.e. at an interest rate, which may be variable or fixed, but which is independent of the performance of the co-operative) and for individual members to receive a capital sum on leaving the co-operative equivalent to their share of its capital value. The former solution rests on the willingness of financial institutions to lend to workers' co-operatives, and may involve relatively high rates of interest. Investment in physical equipment, land and buildings may be favoured since they can be used as collateral for the loan, whereas investment in intangibles (e.g. research and development) is more difficult to finance. In the case of utilities, a supply of finance by government could alleviate some of the difficulties.

The latter solution, by which members leaving the co-operative receive a share of its capital value, has the counterpart that new members have, in effect, to buy a share of the capital value of the co-operative. This could mean rather large sums having to be raised by potential members. In the case of the water industry with a stock market valuation of the order of £25 billion and with a workforce of 40,000, the average sum to be raised would be over £600,000. This could be modified by partial government ownership (with a corresponding interest charge), but the sum would still remain substantial. However, the full effect of paying such an 'entry fee' could be mitigated through mechanisms such as a new member paying the 'entry fee' on a deferred payment basis by accepting a lower money income during a transition period until the equivalent of the entry fee is paid. It should be added that members in a workers' co-operative who, directly or indirectly, pay such an entry fee run some risk that the entry fee may not be returned to them in full in the event of the co-operative being unsuccessful.

Most workers' co-operatives in Britain appear to have adopted the principle of collective ownership. In contrast, the well-known system of workers' co-operatives in Spain, based at Mondragon, adopted the principle of mainly individual ownership:

> collective ownership means that the company's assets are owned by the entire workforce as a group and as a group which changes with time. No individual has the right to draw on and enjoy a personal share of the assets, and he receives no pay-out when he leaves. At Mondragon, on the other hand, up to 70 per cent of all reinvestment is credited to the owner-

> ship of individual workers, and they are paid out in full when they leave. The balance of the assets is held collectively in order to ensure continuity (Anglo-German Foundation for the Study of Industrial Society, 1977, p13).

In the mid 1970s workers were required to put up at least £1000 when joining the group, though this could be done through instalments deducted from wages over a two-year period. Thereafter the worker received their due share of all enterprise profits, though these are normally reinvested in the enterprise on their behalf (p4). Those retiring are paid out their accumulated capital stake, which amounted to some £10,000 to £15,000 in the mid 1970s.

Profession partnerships have some of the attributes of workers' co-operatives, though cannot be considered as workers' co-operatives since only a portion of workers are included (usually the professionally qualified). But those joining a profession partnership will usually have to 'buy themselves in', whether through the payment of a capital sum or through receipt of a lower income than the senior partners over a number of years, which acts as an entry fee. The counterpart is, of course, that there is an exit payment whereby a leaving partner receives his or her share in the capital value of the partnership.

A successful workers' co-operative will build up capital assets, whether in the form of fixed capital equipment, stocks and work-in-progress, or intangible ones such as reputation, or brand name. The capital value of the enterprise is owned collectively by the workers in the co-operative. Selling-out on a collective basis is the mechanism by which workers can 'release' the enterprise capital value (as has been the experience in a number of former workers' co-operatives). As in the case of mutualisation, a legal prohibition would have to be placed on the workers' co-operative being turned into a privately owned corporation.

There can also be a temptation for the current members of a workers' co-operative to begin to hire others on a conventional employment contract, that is for a wage without any entitlement to membership of the co-operative and therefore to a share in its revenue. Incomes of existing members of a co-operative can be seen as a combination of wage and profit, whereas additional workers may be hired for a wage alone, so that the profits which are shared amongst existing members are not diluted by being shared amongst new additional members.

Commitment to co-operative ideals may be sufficient to retain the principle that all who work for the enterprise are members of the co-operative, though the monetary incentive to hire workers remains. Even so there are difficult demarcation decisions to be made: for example, if the enterprise serves a market in which demand fluctuates and hence the requirement for labour varies, what does the workers' co-operative do? Does it bring in workers on a temporary basis and, if so, at what point do they become members? When new members join a workers' co-operative, at what point do they become full members, after serving some form of probation? We cannot hope to resolve those questions here, but would point out that government would need to lay down operating rules for the organisation to ensure that it retained the spirit of a workers' co-operative.

In the context of the future of the privatised utilities and the options for public ownership, workers' co-operatives can be seen as a form of social ownership rather than public ownership. As discussed below, ownership might be formally lodged with government or with the workers collectively, but in either case the workers would have the collective right to the surplus generated by their enterprise. However, workers' co-operatives face a number of difficulties in this context.

First, in so far as the enterprise in question retains a monopoly position, there would still be a requirement for regulation. While worker ownership would have replaced capitalist ownership, many of the reasons for regulation — to restrain exploitation of monopoly power in terms of high prices, to ensure quality of service and the universal supply obligation — would remain. While the use of workers' co-operatives would help to secure some of the objectives for public ownership set out in Chapter 2, it would not accord well with objectives such as public control of the commanding heights of the economy. Workers' co-operatives would (rightly) pursue the interests of their members.

A second difficulty concerns purchasing the assets of the existing privatised utility. There are two broad alternatives here. The first is that the existing work force, acting as a collective, could buy-out the current owners (presumably compulsory). Thus there would be a need to legislate not only to require the current owners to sell their shares, but also to ensure that the existing workers subscribe to the shares purchase. This could be done in the form of a (compulsory) loan by government (or financial institution) to workers, which in turn would be used to purchase the shares. The workers would then be faced with paying interest on the loan, but would receive dividends from their co-operative. In this case, the worker would be a little better off – the dividends would balance out interest payments.

The second alternative is that government purchases the shares of the utility, and then lodges ownership with workers as a collective. Government would then make some charge to the workers' co-operative for the use of the capital assets which it has purchased from the private owners. This would in effect be an interest charge. This differs from the first alternative in that in the first case loans would be made on an individual basis whereas in the second case the loan is in effect made on a collective basis. Provided that the capital sum paid for the purchase of the utility and the interest rate charged are the same, there would be no financial difference for the workers between the two, though there may be a psychological one.

A third difficulty concerns the financing of future investment. As remarked above, there are only two basic options, though in the case being considered this could be opened out to three. These options are: self-financing by the workers' co-operative, borrowing from financial institutions at the given rate of interest, and borrowing from the government. The third option is added here in light of the general reluctance of financial institutions to lend to workers' co-operatives.

Although the utilities, which are our main focus here, are relatively capital-intensive, the relevant issue is their likely need for finance for expansion. The utilities can be considered as relatively mature industries; hence growth for their products is rather subdued. Over the past decade or so, growth rates have been of the order of 3 per cent per annum. Investment requirements have three components: replacement investment (financed by depreciation allowances); capital-deepening (that is increasing the amount of capital equipment for each worker); and capital-broadening. The last of these is linked with the growth of demand, and reflects the need for expansion of productive capacity to meet that growth of demand. Capital-deepening is likely to be relatively unimportant for the utilities. A capitalist enterprise can finance its own investment provided that the rate of profit is greater than the rate of growth of its capital stock. In practice, the capitalist corporation pays out dividends, and it can finance its own investment if the rate of retained profits is greater than the rate of growth of its capital stock.

For a workers' co-operative, the rate of profit has much less meaning (than for a capitalist enterprise). But the workers co-operative can finance its own investment if its surplus after payment of interest charges is greater than its investment requirements. The difficulty which would be faced by a workers' co-operative is that it may be burdened by heavy interest payments. This would arise when (as indicated above) the purchase of the existing capitalist enterprise by a workers' co-operative is financed by borrowing, with the consequent interest charges.

A fourth problem is that legislation on public ownership would need to include two legal measures to ensure that the enterprise remained a workers' co-operative. Firstly – a reflection of a point made above – workers in a co-operative can 'release' the collective capital value of the enterprise as private capital by turning the enterprise into a capitalist corporation. The experience of some privatised companies which were management buy-outs illustrates what can happen: substantial capital gains became available to workers and managers (though those buy-outs differed from workers' co-operatives in that the ownership was on an individual rather than a collective basis). Thus, legal restrictions would need to be placed on the ability of the members of such a co-operative to turn it into a capitalist corporation.

The second legal measure would be to ensure that the workers' co-operative was indeed operated in a democratic and participatory manner. Legislation would therefore be necessary to guarantee that the enterprise was operated on a one member one vote basis, and that all workers were equal members of the co-operative. As noted above, even a broad statement that all workers should be equal members raises issues such as the treatment of part-time workers. The key difference between a workers' co-operative and a capitalist enterprise is that in the former labour hires capital while in the latter capital hires labour. The organisation of the labour process and the rights to any surplus lie with workers collectively rather than with capital. The challenge is to ensure that the collective ownership by workers is translated into democratic participation within the enterprise.

A fifth complication is whether or not a workers' co-operative should be limited in its range of operation, whether geographical or product range. This is a general issue for social ownership, but it has generally been the case that a publicly owned enterprise is limited on both counts. A workers' co-operative would be an autonomous decision-making unit and, as with the privatised utilities, it might very well seek to expand its operations geographically (which would be likely to involve expansion overseas). Similarly, a workers' co-operative might seek to expand the range of goods and services it produces beyond its 'core business'. It might also be the case that a workers' co-operative would only provide the service (gas, electricity or water as the case may be) if it were profitable to do so: here 'profitable' would not mean shareholders having to receive a minimum rate of return, but rather that workers would earn a reasonable income (which would be wages plus dividend).

Finally, there is the question of whether or not investment for workers' co-operatives would be at an adequate level. It was remarked above that there could be some reluctance on the part of workers' co-operatives to invest when this might mean that present income was being sacrificed for future rewards. In the discussion above we indicated ways in which this reluctance could be modified. In the context of workers' co-operatives in the utilities, government might still have to stand ready to lend to the co-operatives if financial institutions prove reluctant to do so.

Concluding remarks

We would suggest that, based on the above arguments, there is no reason for rejecting any of these options on the grounds that they are not feasible or practical. In each case, there would need to be appropriate institutional arrangements made. For example, regional bodies are required for regional public ownership, and financing arrangements would have to be put in place for mutual organisations and workers' co-operatives. As we will discuss in the next chapter, some options may be better suited for some industries than for others, and the options differ in how far they are able to contribute to the objectives outlined in Chapter 2.

8

Conclusions and Recommendations

Introduction

The conclusion which can be drawn from Chapters 3 to 5 is that public ownership is a feasible and attractive option, especially for the utilities. Chapter 3 has surveyed the evidence on the comparative performance of publicly owned companies relative to privately owned ones, and indicated that the perception of inferior performance by publicly owned companies is not confirmed. It also indicated that following privatisation there was only ambiguous improvement in measures such as productivity. Chapter 4 reviewed the difficulties in regulating privatised utilities and suggested that there are numerous problems in ensuring effective regulation. In a narrow sense, public ownership can be viewed as a mode of regulation. In Chapter 5 we reviewed what we termed the practical constraints on public ownership, particularly the utilities. It can be concluded from that chapter that there are no insurmountable constraints on the restoration of public ownership. The idea that there would be costs which would prevent public expenditure on health or education was shown to be largely a myth. There appear to be no measures taken by the European Union which would prevent extension of public ownership, though it is likely that acquisition of private sector assets with little or no compensation would meet legal barriers. The present and evolving structures of the utilities have made the act of taking companies into public ownership more complex than was generally the case with the nationalisation programme of the Attlee government (though probably no more complex than that undertaken by the 1974/79 Labour government).

Options and objectives

We can now review the objectives set out in Chapter 2 in conjunction with our discussion of the six options in Chapter 7, and see how the various options connect with those objectives. We will describe the options of full, strategic and regional public ownership as complete public ownership since all of them would involve 100 per cent state ownership, and as those three options share many characteristics it is useful to group them together in this way.

We begin with the *commanding heights* objective. Complete public ownership would enable there to be control over the commanding heights. Partial public ownership would not ensure that effective control could be exercised to ensure pursuit of the public interest where that conflicts with profits. Workers' co-operatives would not enable public control to be exercised. The case of mutual organisations is less clear cut.

Turning to *community control*, the answers are similar except that mutual organisation in industries where there is universal (or near universal) consumption (and hence membership of the mutual organisation) would also be able to exert community control.

The manner in which *standards of employment* would be affected cannot be fully anticipated as precise effects would depend on objectives set for the organisation and the environment within which it operates. It would, though, seem plausible that partial public ownership and mutual organisation would have least effect, and that the other forms of public ownership, in particular workers' co-operatives, would have greater (beneficial) effect.

We argued that public ownership would not have a major impact on *income and wealth distribution* but could have a beneficial positive impact. Partial public ownership would have little potential for making any impact on the wage and salary or pricing structures. Workers' co-operatives could be expected particularly to have an impact on the wages and salary structure, but little on pricing. It is difficult to foresee the impact which a mutual organisation would have on pricing structure and it is not likely to have any obvious impact on wage and salary dispersion. The other modes of public ownership could potentially have a significant impact on price and wage structures but only if that is made a clear part of the public ownership programme.

Environmental and regulatory considerations could be brought to the fore under the complete public ownership options. This would have to be effected through setting objectives for the public corporations. In the other cases (partial public ownership, mutual organisation and workers' co-operatives), the organisation would continue to have the drive to expand consumption which exists under private ownership.

Cost of capital is in effect lower for the public sector than for the private sector, which imposes a high required rate of return on the investments which it undertakes. Public ownership can draw upon a lower cost of capital to provide lower cost services.

Finally, in terms of regulation, it has been argued that partial public ownership, workers' co-operatives and mutual organisations (though this is less clear cut) would require continuation of regulation where the enterprises concerned retain a natural monopoly position. Full, strategic and regional public ownership could dispense with arms-length regulation of utilities (as practised at present).

A SUMMARY OF THE OPTIONS

Although, as indicated in Chapter 1, public ownership has taken a variety of forms in the past, there tends to be an identification between public ownership and the Morrisonian concept of the nationalised industry. This Morrisonian concept involved complete ownership of a vertically-integrated industry, in which the public corporation would be sole producer. We have set out the options for public ownership in general terms in the preceding chapter. It should be clear from that discussion that there is a wide range of viable options for social ownership, which can be organised on a national, regional or local basis, which may be vertically integrated or not and which may involve collective, consumer, or worker ownership.

It is our general view that there is no single 'best' model for public ownership, and that careful consideration should be given to the different modes of public ownership which may be appropriate for different sectors at different times. It is widely recognised that the water industry, whether under private or public ownership, will continue as a monopoly supplier. In contrast, the current structure of the gas and electricity industries at least raises the question of whether or not a vertically-integrated statutory monopoly would be the appropriate form of public ownership for them.

We could adopt the equivalent of the 'principle of subsidiarity' over the organisational form of public ownership, that is the idea that production and distribution should be organised on the smallest scale and at the most decentralised level, which does not compromise the benefits of economies of scale and of scope and of vertical integration. In the absence of large economies of scale and of substantial transactions costs, organisation of public ownership could be on a small scale with local accountability.

Whatever form of public ownership is recommended, we would suggest that there are three features which must accompany it. First, there must be an appropriate tier of government or other public body to which the public enterprise is clearly accountable. Second, the public enterprise should be operated in the 'public interest' where the nature of that interest is clearly specified in terms of a range of objectives. Third, operation of the public enterprise is clearly based on good employment practices with trade union recognition and involvement following the 'high road' of a highly trained and involved work force rather than the 'low road' of a poorly paid and cowed work force.

We have focused our attention on proposals for public ownership, but these proposals must be considered not only on their own merits but also by comparison with the alternative which is regulated private ownership. We have indicated the shortcomings of regulated private ownership in Chapter 4.

Regulation requires the collection of relevant and accurate information on which price controls and quality of service obligations can be based. Regulation by its nature seeks to regulate and to constrain. In a sense there is regulation in order to prevent private companies from doing what they would have otherwise have done (in this context particularly in the realm of prices). Regulation by its nature does not readily encourage new developments and innovations. In particular, it is difficult to ensure that investment takes place at an adequate rate and provides sufficient capacity to meet the peaks of demand. Regulation involves significant costs, including those of the regulatory agencies as well as the compliance costs for the regulated utilities, and these costs may well increase over time.

THE UTILITIES AND PUBLIC OWNERSHIP

We will conclude by looking at options for the three industries with which UNISON is particularly concerned, namely electricity, gas and water. It should, though, be noted that there has been emerging cross-ownership between different utilities under privatisation. In so far as the reason for this cross-ownership is cost reduction, the structure of public ownership could reflect such potential for cost reduction. An example here could be meter reading and billing: if there are substantial economies in those activities, then a separate company (also publicly owned) could be formed to handle meter reading and billing under contract to the gas and electricity companies.

(i) Electricity industry

When the electricity industry was in public ownership, it could be seen as having four components to its operations: production of electricity, national distribution of electricity, local distribution and supply, and retail outlets. Under privatisation there has been vertical disintegration with (broadly speaking) the four components operated by separate companies (subject to the caveat that some mergers have brought companies operating at different stages back under the same ownership). The four stages differ in that national and local distribution are natural monopolies, and production of electricity is not subject to extensive economies of scale and is increasingly undertaken on a competitive basis. There has been a considerable run down at retail level and the remaining retail outlets of the RECs are in competition with other electrical goods retailers.

Although we have not conducted a detailed study into this, there would not appear to be an imperative for the three stages of production and distribution (that is stages other than retail outlets) or indeed the four stages to be under the same organisational 'umbrella'. Transactions costs involved in the relationships between different stages of production and distribution would not appear to be substantial enough to leave vertical integration as the only option.

Thus it is possible to envisage a number of options for the electricity industry. These would include (as examples) strategic public ownership under which the national grid would be under state ownership; full public ownership of the vertically integrated electricity industry; a mix of strategic (national) public ownership of the national grid, regional government ownership of local electricity distribution and competitive provision of electricity production, some or all of which could be under public ownership. It would also be feasible for any of these stages to be operated as workers' co-operatives, though it would be envisaged that since the national and local distribution would remain natural monopolies there would need to be regulation of their prices. Given the universal usage of electricity, the mutual form of ownership (especially for local distribution) would also be a feasible option.

(ii) Gas industry

Considerations for the gas industry are similar to those for the electricity industry. The natural gas pipeline, for which Transco is currently responsible, acts as both a transmission and distribution network, and is the equivalent of the National Grid for electricity. Thus strategic public ownership would involve the ownership of that network.

There are two differences between the electricity industry and the gas industry which are relevant here. The first is that a substantial minority of people do not receive mains gas supply. While mutualisation would still be feasible, it would not have the same appeal as for those industries where there is universal supply. The second is that the gas industry under both nationalisation and privatisation has been organised on a national rather than regional basis. However, prior to nationalisation the gas industry was structured with production (of town gas) and distribution at the local level with considerable local government involvement. The replacement of town gas by natural gas has meant that domestic production of gas has ceased. Competition has been introduced into the privatised industry on a region by region basis, although this involves supply rather than production of gas. Safety considerations mean that there has to be some regulation over who is permitted to provide gas and use the distribution network.

These remarks would suggest that strategic public ownership of the transmission and distribution network would be one feasible option. It would also be feasible to have regional and full public ownership with a vertically-integrated industry.

(iii) Water industry

There is general agreement that whether the water industry is in private ownership or public ownership it will remain a natural monopoly and the vast majority of consumers will be faced with only one supplier. It would also seem to be the case that the industry will remain a vertically-integrated operation. The main natural monopoly aspect, though, is the distribution of water, and this only requires that there is a single supplier to any particular customer. It does not require that the industry is operated on a nationally-integrated basis. There may be reasons for some form of national water grid so that areas suffering from a water shortage can be aided by water from areas with a water surplus, and hence some agreements between areas would be advantageous, with perhaps a separate national grid.

In the case of the water industry, it is difficult to see how strategic public ownership could be implemented. Otherwise, though, each of the options outlined by UNISON would be viable. Hence the water industry has never been organised on a national basis, and regional public ownership might be a particularly attractive option. In light of the universal use of water, mutualisation would be a viable possibility.

REFERENCES

A. Alchian and H. Demsetz, 'Production, information costs and economic organization', *American Economic Review*, 1972, vol. 62.

Anglo-German Foundation for the Study of Industrial Society, *Worker-owners: the Mondragon Achievement*, London 1977.

M. Bishop, J. Kay and C. Mayer (eds), *The Regulatory Challenge*, Oxford University Press, Oxford 1995.

M. Bishop, J. Kay and, C. Mayer (eds), *Privatization and Economic Performance*, Oxford University Press, Oxford 1994.

R. Bladen-Hovell, 'Fiscal Policy and the Budget' in M. Artis (ed), *The U K Economy* 14th edition, Oxford University Press, Oxford 1997.

A. Boussofiane, S. Martin and D. Parker, 'The impact of technical efficiency of the UK privatization programme', *Applied Economics*, 1997, vol. 29, pp297-310.

H. J. Chang, 'The economics and politics of regulation', *Cambridge Journal of Economics*, 1997, vol. 21, no. 6.

T. Clarke, 'The political economy of the UK privatization programme' in T. Clarke and C. Pitelis (eds), *The Political Economy of Privatization*, Routledge, London 1993.

R. Coase, 'The nature of the firm', *Economica*, vol. 4, 1937;

C. Crosland, *The Future of Socialism*, Cape, London1956.

G. de Fraja, 'In praise of public firms', *New Economy*, vol. 2, no. 3, 1995, pp177-180.

C. Doyle, 'Regulating Firms with Monopoly Power' in R. Sugden (eds), *Industrial Economic Regulation*, Routledge, London 1993.

DTI Press Release, 25 March 1998: information taken from www.coi.gov/coi/depts/ GTI/coi9544d.ok.

J. Fairburn and J. Kay, *Merger and Merger Policy*, Oxford University Press, Oxford 1989.

P. Ferguson, *Industrial Economics: Issues and Perspectives*, Macmillan, London 1988.

B. Fine, 'Scaling the commanding heights of public enterprise economics', *Cambridge Journal of Economics*, 1990, vol. 14, pp127-142.

L. Hannah, 'The economic consequences of the state ownership of industry, 1945-1990' in R. C. Floud and D. N. McCloskey (eds), *The*

Economic History of Britain since 1700, 1994, vol. 3 2nd edition.

D. Helm, 'British utility regulation: theory, practice, and reform', *Oxford Review of Economic Policy*, 1994, vol. 10, no. 3.

G. Holtham, 'Water: our mutual friend', *New Economy*, 1996, vol. 3, no. 4.

W. Hutton, *The State We're In*, Jonathan Cape, London 1995.

S. Littlechild, *Regulation of British Telecommunications' Profitability*, HMSO, London 1983.

S. Marvin, S. Graham and S.Guy, *Privatised Utilities and Regional Management*, South East Economic Development Strategy, Harlow 1996.

R. Millward, 'The nationalised industries' in M. Artis and D. Cobham (eds), *Labour's Economic Policies 1974-79*, Manchester University Press, Manchester 1991.

R. Millward and J. Singleton, *The Political Economy of Nationalisation in Britain, 1920-1950*, Cambridge University Press, Cambridge 1995.

R. Millward, 'The 1940s nationalizations in Britain: means to an end or the means of production ?', *Economic History Review*, 1997, vol. 50, no. 3.

Monopolies and Mergers Commission, *South West Water Services Ltd.*, HMSO, London 1995.

Monopolies and Mergers Commission, *BG plc*, HMSO, London 1997.

L. Morse, 'Co-op utilities, US style', *New Economy*, 1997, vol. 4, no. 4, pp258-261.

Ofwat, *Annual Report, 1996* , HC 21, HMSO, London 1997.

D. Parker, and S. Martin, 'The impact of UK privatization on labour and total factor productivity', *Scottish Journal of Political Economy*, 1995, vol. 42, no.2, pp201-220.

R. Rees and J. Vickers, 'RPI – *X* Price-cap regulation' in Bishop, Kay and Mayer, 1995.

M. Sawyer, *The Economics of Industries and Firms*, Routledge, London 1985.

J. Siraut, 'Putting rail back on track', *New Economy*, 1997, vol. 4, no. 2.

A. D. Smith, and D.M.W.N. Hitchens, and S.W. Davies, *International Industrial Productivity Comparisons of Britain, America and Germany*, Cambridge University Press, Cambridge 1982.

G. Stigler, 'The theory of economic regulation', *The Bell Journal of Economics and Management Science*, 1971, vol. 2.

J. Tomlinson, 'Is successful regulation possible: some theoretical issues' in R. Sugden (eds), *Industrial Economic Regulation*, Routledge, London 1993.

Trade and Industry Committee, *Second Report, Progress in the Liberalisation of the Gas Market*, HC 338, January 1998.

Treasury, *Pre Budget Report*, Cmnd. 3804, HMSO, London 1997.

UNISON, *The Privatised Utilities*, Unison, London 1996.

J. Vickers and G. Yarrow, *Privatization: An Economic Analysis*, MIT Press, 1989.

C.Waddams Price, 'Regulating for fairness', *New Economy*, 1997, vol. 4 no. 2, pp117-122.

O.E. Williamson, *The Economic Institutions of Capitalism*, Free Press, New York 1985.

G. Yarrow, 'Privatization in Theory and Practice', *Economic Policy*, 1986, pp324-377.